CORDON BLEU CHRISTIANITY

A COLLECTION OF SERMONS

BY

DAVID SHEPHERD

MEADOWSIDE PUBLICATIONS
DUNDEE
2005

Meadowside Publications
14 Albany Terrace, Dundee DD3 6HR

Printed by
Prontaprint
Dundee, Scotland

ISBN: 978-0-9551974-0-6

Meadowside Religion
is a © imprint of
Meadowside Publications,
Dundee

CONTENTS

Introduction

For several years, people have suggested that I should give my sermons a wider circulation than the pulpit or the church magazine. They have doubtless felt that they would have infinitely more value than my detective novels. But it is only through that experience of self-publishing, that I have gained sufficient confidence to produce this book.

In the course of an active ministry, I have written over 1200 sermons – and given 800 funeral addresses. I have therefore selected thirty-two of my favourite pieces which aim to teach as well as to entertain.

I am, of course, conscious that most of these sermons have been written after asking for the help and guidance of the Holy Spirit. How often I have stared at a blank sheet of paper or gone round the house, looking at other people's sermons and then slamming the books back into their shelves in sheer frustration. I must therefore express my gratitude that many desperate prayers have so frequently been answered – and so often at the last moment!

I am also very grateful to those inspired and inspiring preachers whom I have listened to throughout my life. I would also like to say a word of thanks to all the dreadful preachers I have had to endure – those whose half-baked offerings have presented the glorious Christian faith in its most dismal and incoherent forms. They too have spurred me on to do better.

Finally, I would like to thank the congregations of St Paul's Cathedral, Dundee, and my own St Mary Magdalene's who have given me their constant encouragement and a fair hearing through a long and perhaps controversial ministry. I would like to thank Gill and Roger Ellis and Linda and Bryn Richardson who wanted to see this book "done" and also the staff of Prontaprint and Judey Struth who have helped to turn so many dreams into printed reality.

No book would be complete without a generous tribute to my hard-working wife, Patricia, and her family who have provided the love, support and comfort in which to write – both the sacred and the profane!

David Shepherd

29th August 2005

Why Sermons?

According to St Luke, when Jesus preached his first sermon in Nazareth, the people there tried to kill him. I have – thus far – been spared such violence; but I have had my full share of criticism.

I well remember my third sermon in the Cathedral. As was customary in those days, I handed it over to Provost Haggart. He returned it with some complimentary remarks. It was very well written, he said. Beautiful language. The congregation would love it. But . . . a significant pause . . . "I'm not going to let you preach it!" I was shocked. "Why not?" "Because it says absolutely nothing!" I grew up in a hard school.

On another Sunday – during my sermon – the Provost decided that the loud-speaker system was not working properly. So, during my spell in the pulpit, I had to contend with electronic squeaks and whistles, zzzing and buzzing. I don't know what it did to the congregation, but it quite unnerved me. At the end of the service, I descended on Provost Haggart and said with some anger: "I hope you'll never do that again. You absolutely mangled my sermon!" He looked at me with his cold, grey eyes. "It deserved to be mangled!"

I say all this because sermons can be the most controversial parts of the service. People have said to me: "That was absolute rubbish!" Whilst someone else – speaking about the same sermon – will say: "Thank you. I found that most helpful." One learns quickly that one man's meat is another man's poison.

Bishop Luscombe tells the story of a sermon during Evensong at St Margaret's, Newlands, in Glasgow. The sermon was so boring that he started adding up the numbers on the hymn board. Whilst he was doing this, it suddenly came to him that God was calling him to be a priest. So perhaps the sermon had some value after all?

Why do we preach sermons? Well, in the Jewish synagogue tradition, when a passage had been read from scripture, it was customary for someone to explain what the reading was all about. The passage that Jesus was expounding came from Isaiah, chapter 61. The thing which infuriated his audience was that Jesus said the prophecy referred to himself. He was the long-expected Messiah, but they couldn't accept it.

After Pentecost, the apostles were obliged to preach in order to explain who this person Jesus was; why he had been crucified; how God had raised him from the dead. And then inviting their hearers to be baptized and receive themselves the gift of the Holy Spirit. Reading through the book of Acts, we discover that most of the early apostles were pretty poor preachers. St Peter's sermon at Pentecost was dire! And yet, we are told, as a result of his preaching, no less than 3000 people were converted in one day.

Perhaps, considering the present failure of the Church

to make any impact on society, we might say: "sermons don't work." But when one discovers the level of ignorance amongst Christian people – particularly in their knowledge of the Bible, one might suggest that there is a strong case for longer and more profound sermons. I remember one lady in St Mary Magdalene's – a member of the Vestry – who couldn't find St Luke! And an assistant priest – no names mentioned – who didn't know where to find the pastoral epistles of St John. We need more sound teaching.

Bishop Forbes wrote a book of sermons entitled: "Are you being converted?" In his time, sermons lasted an hour. When I first went to the Cathedral in 1968, the average length was 25 minutes. My 12 – 15 minutes was considered a bit short. People felt they weren't getting their money's worth. It took only three Polo mints, not the usual six!

If sermons seem an ordeal to you, consider the plight of the poor preacher! He – or she – has probably spent an hour or two thinking about the sermon. They have scribbled ideas down on paper; crossed them out; consulted books; perhaps even prayed for guidance – and received it! Hesitatingly – but lovingly – they have typed the whole thing out, knowing full well the mockery and criticism they will receive.

There will be black looks from the choir when they see the sheaf of notes. People will look at their watches to see how long he or she will be this morning.

They will be only too willing to moan if the preacher makes them too late to catch their buses. Some will say they are too deaf to hear a word. Others will declare that even though they heard every word perfectly clearly, the message went in one ear and came out of the other. With a universal sigh of relief, everyone will rise to their feet to say the Creed. The preacher's lot is not a happy one!

But it is, you know, the one creative act in the service. The Liturgy, the music, the prayers, the hymns have all been said or sung many times before. The sermon should be completely fresh. Of course, we have known preachers who have torn pages out of books of sermons and read them to their people. In Elizabethan times, several books of homilies were produced so that, even if the clergy were a bit dim, they could at least read out something intelligent to their people. One has to remember that going into a pulpit is not something that anyone does lightly. It is always a bit of an ordeal – even for an experienced preacher.

The story is told of a young curate who flounced into the pulpit to deliver his first sermon. With great pride and enthusiasm, he waved his arms in wild gestures and declaimed his message with great gusto. Sadly, in the course of his sermon, he swept all his notes off the pulpit on to the floor. He came to a grinding halt. He couldn't think of anything to say. He crept down the steps in abject shame. After the service was over, the verger said to him: "If you'd gone up the way you came down, you'd have come down the way you went up!"

What do we aim to preach? First of all, we try to focus on the latest events. To consider how they affect us as people. How we, as Christians, should react. Secondly, we expound the scriptures in the hope that, by explaining them, we may understand our faith better – and make it more effective. Sometimes, we have to criticize. I have only had to rebuke this congregation a few times during my period as Rector. I do it with some reluctance. I know it is hard to take criticism from a friend. But sometimes, it has to be done.

I have told you before of a Sunday morning just after Christmas when I was peacefully eating my cornflakes and fully intending to use an old sermon. Suddenly it came to me that I must write a new sermon – a very blunt sermon.

The words came to me quicker than I could write them down. It was an attack on the congregation for their dismal attendance at Christmas. I firmly believe that that sermon came from head office. It was pretty rough and there was a lot of resentment afterwards. But it needed to be said. And it still needs to be repeated. Because the attendance of this congregation at Christmas midnight and on Christmas morning is a disgrace.

A sermon should stimulate our minds. It should encourage us to think. To read more ourselves. To dig deeper. To act more confidently. To be better Christians. If a sermon does not stimulate, the best thing to do is to tell the preacher what you thought was wrong with it. If you put up with rubbish, you have only yourselves to blame!

Hopefully, in St Mary Magdalene's, we do keep you interested. And awake! But, sometimes, it is up to the people to help their priest to be a better preacher. We need encouragement too. And, very often, it is a helpful word of criticism – rather than a vague word of praise – which can spur us to try harder . . . to do better.

However, if you do get so frustrated, so angry, as the Jews did in Nazareth when Jesus was preaching, and you feel like stoning us as we come through the church door, it is possible you may have left things too late! I draw comfort from the fact that – unlike St Paul – my preaching has never landed me in jail! But I suppose there is still time!

(19th June 2005)

Cordon Bleu Christianity

During the course of my visits, I often find myself sitting in people's kitchens; and I cannot help noticing how many ladies in the congregation seem to have cookery books by Delia Smith. They have watched her on television and have gone out to buy her books. Presumably they have also had a stab at following her recipes. Thus, when they have set about creating haggis stroganoff or black pudding in aspic, they have doubtless kept her book open at the appropriate page and followed her instructions to the letter.

For any recipe, you have to have the right ingredients and follow the correct order of preparation to get the best results. When you know the recipe, it is always possible to introduce a few variations and cut a few corners; but for the best results – indeed, to have any results at all – you have to follow the instructions laid down in the book.

Now what is true of Delia Smith and her cooking is true of our Christian life.

Many people think they can walk into the Christian kitchen, select any ingredients they fancy, cook them in any way they like and then expect that the end product will be a raving success! The truth is that such actions lead to total chaos. You cannot fry jelly! You cannot bake without flour. And yet, people try to live what they call a Christian life with none of the essential ingredients which, in God's eyes, is completely stupid.

If you are going to make a success of something, you must follow the book. You copy a pattern. And the closer you approximate to the pattern, the more likely you are to see a satisfactory result emerge. Presumably, if you set about cooking stuffed aubergines, that is what you want to eat? Presumably, if you set out to be a Christian man or woman, that is what you want to be? If not, why bother?

I say that because when we baptize children, we are not just performing a symbolic act. We are initiating a Christian life; making that small person part of the Christian family; setting them out on the road that leads to heaven and eternal life. For each child, there is a long way to go and many vital ingredients will be needed if that child is to grow properly as a Christian person.

Children are born chaotic. They learn order and discipline. They seek examples and patterns. They copy us. They have to be told what is right and wrong. On important matters, they cannot be allowed to pick and choose. They have to be steered firmly in the right direction. Like a small ship crossing a great ocean, a close eye has to be kept on the compass. Constant shifts of the rudder to maintain course and speed. But which course should they follow? What pattern should they adopt?

As Christian people, we say that we should follow Jesus. He is, as the Christmas carol puts it – our childhood pattern. And just as his life as a son of God began with baptism, so our life with God begins with water. Not in the River Jordan but in the font at the west end of the church. And the pattern goes on from there.

Jesus did not live out his life in isolation. He lived it in the company of others. With his disciples. They ate together; talked together; travelled on the same road. One of the essential parts of Christian life is that we meet together on Sundays and join in prayer and worship together. Only when we assemble the right ingredients will good things begin to happen.

If you have a solitary egg sitting on a plate, it's not likely to do all that much. But, break it up, mix it with flour, put in the sugar, start stirring . . . and you're getting somewhere. In the same way, the Christian man, woman or child needs to be taken out of their isolation, broken, spread, mixed with others and really stirred up before good things start to happen.

You cannot be a Christian in isolation. You cannot be a Christian without going to Church. (Did you ever meet a sailor who never went to sea? Or a fisherman who never went fishing? Of course not!) We have to participate actively in the Christian community. We have to lose something of our individuality . . . our selfishness. What we have has to be shared with others. The richness of our Christian life depends on what we put into the mixing bowl and what we receive from the input of others. Our talents. Our faith. That is what makes a church rich!

The more we give of ourselves, the richer is our offering to God. If we give God only the equivalent of one egg, one grain of sugar, one smear of flour – he is scarcely likely to make a great cake! In fact, he is hardly likely to make anything! In cooking, we can see the point. But when it comes to churches, people are blind. We assume that we can have a great church, a great Christian community, something splendid and wonderful, for little or no effort on our part.

God can certainly do a lot with a little; but if all we give him are the dregs of our time, money and commitment, there will be no miracle. You will remember that it was only when the disciples provided Jesus with the contents of their lunch box that Jesus was able to feed the 5000. Jesus needed the complete offering of the disciples before a miracle could take place.

No lunch box; no miracle!

We are basically very selfish people. We all prefer to go our own way; do our own thing. But that does not lead us to heaven. It leads to trouble. At the Last Supper, Jesus said to his disciples: "Do this in remembrance of me." But we don't do it.

Jesus said: "If a man wishes to be my disciple, let him take up his cross and follow me." We say: "I prefer to snuggle under my downie." Jesus said: "This is the first and greatest commandment. You shall love the Lord your God with all your heart, with all your soul, with all your mind and all your strength." But over half the congregation say: "Sod off, mate! I've got my own life to lead."

And that is it – until the day of the funeral when all the family stands weeping and sobbing, saying: "Lord Jesus, remember little Sidney. He didn't do much for you; but he was a member of the Boy's Brigade. Surely you wouldn't refuse him?"

By that time it is probably too late!

Proper cooking – and proper Christianity – means following the book. Leaving out of our cooking all those things which spoil a good recipe: sin, the world, the flesh and the devil. Putting in the proper ingredients: love, joy, peace, forgiveness, service, sacrifice, worship, prayer, sacraments. All good stuff! Mixing them together usefully in a Christian community. Making something deliciously rich and tasty which will attract others. Making our life resemble that of Jesus.

Not just for one day in our lives. But every day. Becoming Cordon Bleu Christians, who have the Word of Life at their finger tips. A well-stocked larder of Christian grace. A well-equipped kitchen, prepared for any eventuality. If Delia can do it, so can we!

(10th July 1983)

Happy Families?

When I was a child, one of my favourite card games was "Woodland Happy Families" with those beautifully painted scenes by Racey Helps – Mr Badger and Mrs Badger, Master Owl and Miss Owl. And one grew up psychologically conditioned to think that the ideal family consisted of a father, mother and two children – one of each sex. Added to this was a cat or a dog, which are felt – by some people – to be essential ingredients for a happy family. Well, we had a dog – but no sister! The dog had to be put down because of old age and, shortly afterwards, my father died! So we weren't really much of a family.

A family is part of a tribal system – especially here in Scotland. If you were a Macdonald, you were perhaps a Macdonald of Clanranald. You knew who you were and where you came from. A family gave you identity. It gave you protection. And when you married, that other person was brought into your family.

We are told that, today, the concept of family is under attack. Strangely, when I was writing this address, I had just been reading William Temple's book: "Christianity and the Social Order" (written in 1942) where he says that the ideal of the family was under attack – then. So, nothing changes?

But today, we are beginning to see families in a different light. Not as Mr and Mrs Badger but as any combination of folk who live together and care for each other.

It might be two men . . . two women . . . It might be one woman, one child . . . one man with two children . . . Or perhaps like Woody Alien and Mia Farrow in happier times, when they had no less than 12 or 14 adopted children from all sorts of races and colours – all part of one rich and diverse family.

What kind of family is the Christian supposed to uphold? Which one is the Christian supposed to condemn? A homosexual couple who provide warmth and love? Or a supposedly 'normal' family where there are bitter tensions and quarrels – the father violent and angry; the mother weeping and anxious; everyone living permanently on the brink of divorce? One outwardly ideal. The other apparently irregular.

I was brought up very much in a one-parent family (which may explain a lot!) I have grown up without any children of my own. For some years, six University students living at the Rectory constituted my family. We are often worried that if a child does not have a normal family upbringing, it will suffer. I do not believe this to be true.

Some families are very narrow and exclusive. They can be claustrophobic. But others have an open door. Under pressure, they gladly expand like an accordion. But there is nothing more selfish than the typical 'normal' family, living to itself, for itself, behind locked doors.

Families are not always happy institutions. They fight. They quarrel. People hate their brothers. Sisters do not speak to each other for years. Parents are brow-beaten and trampled upon by their fearsome offspring. Children run away from home to escape domineering mothers. Others despise their fathers for being failures. There is a lot that is sad in a family.

The Old Testament contains a disastrous record of family life. People are constantly at war with each other. Cain kills his brother, Abel. Jacob deceives his brother, Esau. Joseph was persecuted by ten of his brothers, thrown into a pit and sold into slavery! We shall not look to the Bible to find the ideal family. In fact, the word "family" is only mentioned once in the New Testament. I was surprised at that; but I should not have been.

The Holy Family, the focus of our Christmas celebrations, was not all it might have been. Jesus was not Joseph's child. Mary and Joseph were definitely not married when Jesus was born. They were very similar to many dysfunctional families today. They may look an ideal family on the front of a Christmas card, but I would imagine – in Bethlehem – there were many deep and difficult problems waiting to be sorted out.

When he began his ministry, Jesus said to his disciples: "If anyone wishes to follow me, let him give up his father and mother and wife and children and brothers and sisters, yes, and even his own life – and follow me!" Not exactly the ideal recipe for family life! Later, when he was reminded of his own family connections; told that his mother and brothers had come to see him; what did he say? He said: "Who is my mother and who are my brothers?" And reaching out his hands to those about him – the brown faces, the broken teeth and the smelly feet – he said: "You are my mother and my brothers. For whoever does the will of my Father in heaven, the same is my brother, sister and mother!" Difficult words!

From which, we gather that Jesus did not think of the Christian family as the sum total of lots of little families; but rather a series of broken pieces which on their own look lost and jagged – but which find unity and meaning only in God.

So, I suppose we are fortunate in this congregation that we do not represent a conglomeration of happy, little families. We seek them; but they constantly elude us. As anyone who looks closely at our congregation will realize, the family that worships together here is a rare bird indeed. We are much more like the Christian family that Jesus intended his church to be. Very much a collection of broken bits.

No natural geographical affinity. We come from all corners of the city – and beyond. Some of us are bereaved; some divorced; some separate. Some of us are one-parent families; some widows; some rich; some poor. Some of us are happy; others sad. We are a complete mixture.

And, hopefully, in this family – this Christian family – we find healing; we find warmth, love and acceptance. We are welcomed for what we are. The jagged, painful bits no longer stick out like sore thumbs. The emptiness is filled. Our defects no longer matter quite so much. We find that in God – and with our Christian brothers and sisters, we have a value and an importance which we have nowhere else in this world.

We are not just a number here. Not a case to be dealt with; nor an item on a computer screen. But a valued, cherished person who has their own special place in this family. We are no longer alone. In the Body of Christ, we find a real family – a real home.

(26th October 1997)

Christ!

Of all the commandments, it is No.3 which has recently caused the most stir. And if you don't believe me, ask Mr Salman Rushdie! He wrote a gently mocking book, called "The Satanic Verses", poking fun at the Moslems' idea of God and he was promptly accused of blasphemy. A price was put on his head – and blessed is the man who tops him! As a result of which, Mr Rushdie has lived a very sheltered life for the past five years, because both Moslems and Jews take this commandment very seriously.

What does the commandment actually say? It says: "You shall not take the Name of the Lord your God in vain; for the Lord will not hold him guiltless who takes his Name in vain." Quite simple really. God's name is holy – and is to be treated with respect. The name of the other gods didn't matter because those gods were not real. They couldn't do anything to touch you. You could praise them – or curse them – to your heart's content and they wouldn't blink an eyelid. But the God of Abraham, Isaac and Jacob was different.

Very quickly, the children of Israel discovered that this God was real. He responded rapidly to human beings.

When they asked for help, they got it. When they were disobedient, a divine thunderbolt swiftly followed! You didn't muck around with this God! You treated him with extreme caution. Before approaching him, you were well-advised to observe the little notice attached to every electricity pylon: "Danger! High Voltage."

So the third commandment was not written lightly – or without a great deal of experience. It was a distinct warning to future generations. People knew what happened to people who took the Name of the Lord in vain. Whole communities had suffered from the impiety of one man. Blasphemy was therefore made a capital offence. In the book of Leviticus, we read: "He who blasphemes the Name of the Lord shall be put to death. All the congregation shall stone him." A visitor as well as a native Jew. "When he blasphemes the Holy Name, he shall be put to death."

Mr Rushdie may well have thought he was living in a different age. But there are still those who take the commandments very seriously. What then was this name of the Lord which was so precious? Unfortunately no one knew! They treated God's name with such respect – and with such awe – that before long, only a few priests dared to utter it. And because they didn't tell anyone, it was soon a complete mystery. So, as Victor Gollancz, the publisher, once put it, we have a God of a Thousand Names. Allah, Dieu, Gott, Bog, Jahweh, Jehovah – and all the rest. Every nation has its own name.

But it is not so much the name that matters. It is the person behind the name. For the way we speak about God shows the way we feel about him. If we use his name as a swear word, it shows we have absolutely no idea of the person we are abusing. If we did know, we wouldn't dare do it.

When people say: "Christ!" as they hit their thumb with a hammer or drop a Le Creuset pan on their big toe, it is perhaps bearable because the word Christ is simply the Greek word for "Messiah." But to anyone who believes that Jesus is not just the Messiah but God himself, it is again not a word lightly to be used. It is a word we use in almost every prayer we make; "Through Jesus Christ our Lord."

We cannot use the same word to approach God – and to curse him. It is always painful to Christian people to hear the name of someone they hold precious – used thoughtlessly and as a term of abuse. Perhaps the attitude of Moslems towards blasphemy may give the world pause for thought. And it may be that, sheltering under their righteous indignation, people may once again be compelled to treat God with the respect he deserves.

One thing is certain sure. God is not devalued or destroyed by our blasphemy. But man is . . . poisoned by his own contempt . . . choked with his own filth. As Jesus said: "It is not what goes into a man which defiles him, but what comes out . . . " Can a bad tree produce good fruit? Can a polluted well provide clean water? Do men gather grapes from thistles? Obviously not! The way we speak about God shows clearly the way we feel about him. We demonstrate either our devotion – or the rottenness within.

Well, you may say, that's got nothing to do with me. I don't blaspheme. But there is another way in which we break this third commandment. And that is by trivializing the Holy Name. By letting what we say just run off our tongues without thinking what we are saying. Prayer must never be idle gabble. That is why we take the prayers slowly in St Mary Magdalene's. We try to think about what we are actually saying. "Our Father . . . Our . . . Father. " It's a wonder we ever reach the end of that prayer. We could spend ten minutes thinking about each bit!

Our danger as Christian people is failing to realize the power of the Holy Name. I have prayed with many people and often asked for healing in the name of Jesus. I have dealt with people who seemed possessed and commanded that an evil spirit come out of them. The results have often surprised me. Sometimes even frightened me. But I have never hesitated to invoke the power of the Trinity – and that invocation has brought positive results.

It has convinced me that God does hear exactly what we say. As the children of Israel discovered the hard way: "the eyes of the Lord are over the righteous and his ears are open to their prayer." God knows when we take his name in vain. When we treat it with familiarity or contempt. He can see our faith grow cold. Our tone of voice is an apt demonstration of our feelings.

So let us not take the Name of God lightly. His Name is one of power for good and evil. Let us make sure we use it properly – for our own good and for the benefit of those for whom we pray. That God will hear our words and turn our prayers into healing both in body and spirit. "May the words of our mouths and the thoughts of our hearts be acceptable in thy sight, O Lord, our strength and our Redeemer."

(August 1994)

24

The Right Man For The Job

During the past week, all the clergy and lay representatives in the Diocese have received a memo from the Primus, giving us a timetable for the forthcoming episcopal election. Anyone can be nominated; but only three or four individuals will be shortlisted.

The Pharisee, in our Gospel for this morning, would (at first sight) seem a good choice. He is a man of prayer. Perhaps his prayers are a little one-sided; but he is certainly in touch with the Almighty! Being a Pharisee, he is of course an educated man, well-versed in Jewish Law, and (it goes without saying) he is a man of exemplary behaviour.

He doesn't hesitate to remind us that he is a cut above the rest. He is not grasping. He has a fine understanding of what is right. He has no sexual failings. (What a relief!) He is morally perfect. He fasts – not just once a week – but twice a week! (Which puts us all to shame.) And he gives 10% of his income to the Church.

A generous man. A treasurer's dream! He might be that rare sort of bishop who would refuse to take a higher wage than any of his clergy. (That would certainly help

25

struggling churches to pay their Quota!)

Faced with his name on the ballot paper, we might very well say: "Yes. He's the ideal man for the job." Whereas the other character – the publican . . . Well, he is obviously a non-starter!

By profession, he is a tax-collector. (Need we say more?) Even as a non-stipendiary, he would be a bit of a liability. He freely admits to being a sinner. So guilty, he can hardly look God in the face. His crimes distress him – and so they should! If the *Sun* or the *Daily Record* were to rumble him, just think of the ensuing publicity! So he is obviously out of the Episcopal stakes! No hope there!

But – strangely – Jesus commends the publican. Not for his potential as a bishop; but for his honesty . . . his awareness of his failings . . . his willingness to repent.

As a man who understands that God is a God of forgiveness and love, he is a man who is justified. (That is the key word.) A man who is accounted righteous in the sight of God. Just the sort of person Jesus came to save. When you think about it, he was another St Peter.

For wasn't it Peter who said: "Depart from me, O Lord, for I am a sinful man?" And yet, he went on to become an apostle, a martyr, the first bishop of the Church in Rome and churches have been named after him all over the world. Or perhaps another St Paul – the murderer – who told his readers in Corinth: "I was not worthy to be called an apostle because I persecuted the Church of God?" So perhaps there is a place for sinners after all?

Certainly, the Pharisee had many gifts. But he lacked humility. Many people who exercise positions of power lack humility. Raised to high office in Church and State, they forget who they are – what they are. They see themselves as they want to be seen; but perhaps they are already on the slippery slope. Enoch Powell once reminded us: "Every political career ends in tears."

God prefers the publican; because there is an open door between them. The publican will always turn to God in his moment of need. So God has more chance of helping him. But the Pharisee is totally self-sufficient. He doesn't need other people. He doesn't even need God. Talented, able, teflon-coated, he despises the poor, the ignorant, the social misfits. We see that, even whilst he is praying, he is busy running down his fellow-worshipper. I am better than he is . . . I have better clothes than he has . . . My daughter has a degree from Oxford . . . His son is unemployed . . .

Christians very often stray into dangerous territory – becoming Pharisees. We judge. But it is a risky business. For if God judges us, we have had it. Pride, ambition, selfishness creep through us like dry rot creeping through a building.

I remember preaching a sermon on humility at the Cathedral. In my youthful arrogance, I felt moved to say: "I'm really a very humble person." After the service, Provost Haggart said: "It was a pity you had to say so!" Even in humility, there can be foolish pride.

So let us be careful. Even though the Pharisee would look fine sitting on his episcopal throne, and the picture in the next day's *Courier* would look impressive, this is not how God sees things. St Paul, in his letter to the Christians in Phillipi, says this:

"Let this mind be in you as it was in the Lord Jesus;

Who – even though he was in the form of God – did not count equality with God a thing to be grasped; But he humbled himself; took upon himself the likeness of a servant – and accepted even death on a cross."

St Paul is saying that if even Jesus could show such humility, so should we. We do not belong to a monarchical church – or a totalitarian church – where the top people lord it over the rest of us. Even though we do have bishops, we are a servant church. And every pope, every bishop, every priest is first and foremost a deacon – one who serves. Every Christian engaged in ministry should remember that our priorities are to worship God and to serve mankind in all its suffering and need. If we forget that – any of us – our ministry will be doomed.

St Paul said: "We have this treasure in earthen vessels to remind us that the transcendent power belongs to God and not to us." And a few verses earlier, he says: "For what we preach is not ourselves, but Jesus as Lord – with ourselves as your servants for Christ's sake." This is the sort of Church I wish to belong to. That is the sort of Christian I want to be.

(17th October 2004)

All Cretans Are Liars!

This is not my own personal opinion. I have never met anyone from Crete. It is a statement from one of St Paul's epistles. We are told that the Bible is the Word of God – so it must be true. "All Cretans are liars . . . !" Perhaps we should make discreet enquiries as to whether our own beloved Prime Minister was born in Crete!

However, it does highlight the dangers of taking the Bible too literally. In the Church of England, as we know, there is a dreadful hoo-haa about what the Word of God says to the Church about gay priests. To me, it suggests a terrible misunderstanding about the nature of God . . . and a quite unpardonable misuse of Scripture.

If we were to follow the teaching of the Old Testament (where the Evangelicals get most of their ammunition), every Christian male would be circumcised. None of us would eat pork – out go bacon and sausages! No mussels, no oysters, no crabs! And certainly no haggis!

Anyone committing adultery or fornication would die. Unmarried mothers would be stoned on their front doorsteps. Women would not be allowed to wear jeans – or men to wear skirts. (Bad news for the clergy.) You, as a congregation, would automatically give 10% of your income to the Church. There are very few verses about homosexuals in the Bible; but you can probably guess what the Law says about them; they must be killed!

If you are going to say: "Every word in the Bible is true . . . " or "Every word is the Word of God and must be obeyed . . . " there are going to be some fearsome changes in the laws of England and Scotland. You just cannot quote a section of Jewish law to reinforce a prejudice.

You will recall that St Paul did his best to stop Gentile Christians being circumcised. He said it wasn't necessary. The Law was wrong. Similarly, when Jesus was asked which foods were "unclean", he said that it wasn't the food that went into a person which defiled them; but the poison that came out. Jesus forgave the woman taken in adultery. Everybody else wanted to stone her. He said: "Go and sin no more."

It is perfectly clear that the New Testament dispenses with the Law of Moses. It changes the rules. Now there are just two commandments. Love God . . . and love your neighbour. What is quite clear is that we cannot run the Christian Church on the basis of the Jewish Law. If we were Jews, fair enough. But we are Christians; we follow Christ. We forgive. "How often shall my brother sin against me and I forgive him? Till seven times?" "I say to you until seventy times seven."

That is the difference.

The New Testament is radically different. We cannot graft on the Jewish Law and say: "This is Christianity!" We cannot say that the Word of God is engraved in stone and cannot be changed. Heavens above! That is precisely what the Pharisees said 2000 years ago. And it was the

Pharisees who plotted to kill Jesus.

So my first point in this current row, which is tearing the Church apart, is that we should not misuse Scripture. Even though we call it the Holy Bible, it is not a holy book. For instance, the book of Genesis is full of sin and crime. It is worse than the *News of the World*. I would hesitate to let any child read the book of Genesis for fear of the ideas it would put into their minds.

What the Bible does show us is how God reveals himself to us – despite the sin, despite the horror. A God of Love fighting against the odds to save mankind from the powers of darkness. And some of that darkness is religious darkness . . . spiritual blindness . . . what St Paul called: "Spiritual wickedness in heavenly places."

Whatever sins Dr John, the proposed bishop, may have committed is as nothing when compared to the bigotry and persecution launched against him – which is frightening.

What sort of God do they think they are worshipping? A God of fear and punishment? Surely after 2000 years of Christianity we should know better? The God I worship has a sense of humour. He is understanding, patient, interested, helpful, joyful, glorious. He knows our faults, our mistakes, but he tries to help us through them. He does not condemn anyone.

He is trying to sanctify human nature; to bring us up to heaven; to make us see the beauty of life; the value of every human being. The unmarried mum, the asylum seeker, the pompous civil servant, the gay priest, the unwanted foetus, the homeless drunk – even George Best!

God does not exclude anyone. He welcomes us all as we are. Mucky, muddled, mis-shapen, he enfolds us in the arms of his love. "Whilst we were yet sinners, Christ died for us . . . " Give thanks to God that our Church – the Scottish Episcopal Church – is an inclusive Church. We have got to understand – 2000 years on – that our God is different. He is not the God of the Old Testament, the God of rules and regulations. He is the God of mercy and of grace.

This means that we do not treat people like lepers. Have the critics of Dr John never read the parable in Matthew 25? "Lord, when did we see you a stranger and welcome you?" "When did we see you as a gay priest and persecute you?"

We have spent years – years – hammering home the message that, as Christians, we respect other people whatever their colour, race, gender, religion or sexuality. In Christ, we are all one. Nobody is outside his love or his care. God needs all sorts of Christians to minister to the world. For him, their sexuality is not an issue. Our God is moving on. And we are moving on to fresh challenges. To new understanding. To greater compassion.

One of the great mistakes of the Bible thumpers is to think that the Bible ends with the Book of Revelation. What about the Holy Spirit? Has He gone into retirement these past 2000 years? God's revelation of Himself goes on.

And we have to keep up with the mighty wind of the Holy Spirit. As Jesus challenged the Pharisees of his day – and as St Paul challenged the misconceptions of the Early Church, so God's most Holy Spirit challenges us –

through all these debates and conflicts. In the scale of Divine Love and human compassion, where do we stand? With the loving God? Or with the persecutors baying for blood?

What matters – for all of us – is not our sexuality, but our Christianity. How we respond to God. How we treat other people. There is a place in heaven . . . a place in the Church . . . for Dr John and many others. But, of course, if he was a Cretan, there would be no hope for him at all!

(15th July 2003)

Am I My Brother's Keeper?

When someone falls ill in the congregation, members of the family – quite naturally – ask me to remember that person in our prayers. For as long as they are in hospital, that duty is gladly carried out. in fact, we usually continue to pray for them as they convalesce at home for at least another two or three weeks. They are remembered at each service and the congregation are asked to take away at least one name to be included in their own private prayers at home.

Thus, whilst Mr X or Mrs Y is ill, they are supported by a vast hammock of prayer – everyone contributing their little piece – which, woven together by God, holds up and sustains both the sick person and all those who look after them. The importance of this mutual support in prayer should not be underestimated.

Now this is not just something a clergyman does. It is a function carried out by the whole Christian community. We come to Church to worship God but we also come to pray for each other – even for people we do not know – that God may heal the sick, the depressed, the broken and the dying. And I know from personal experience how much the prayers of faithful people do help and encourage the sick and their families.

So often, when tragedy or sickness occurs, it is difficult to pray clearly for oneself. One is too involved. At that moment, it is good to know that there is a great body of people behind you, doing what at that moment you cannot do yourself.

What does worry me is that people so often expect our prayers for their loved ones, but seem to forget that every week there are other people also needing their help and support. Too often, when one's own family is blooming, the spirit of "I'm all right, Jack!" takes over. "Why should I bother to go to church this morning?" we say. "I don't need anything from God." But, every week, some other poor sod is needing your help and, if they don't get it, the burden of responsibility lies partly on you.

To neglect your duty to be present and pray for others is a sin of omission which is just as bad as a sin of commission. We may say: "Well, I didn't know she was ill!" But why didn't we know? Jesus told his disciples to watch and pray. Absent Christians are not very good watchmen.

You might well say: "Why doesn't God do something for the sick people himself?" Why wait for us and our pathetic little prayers? The answer to these two questions is that we are partners with God in the work of Creation. We have been given responsibility for our fellow men. God means us to take up that responsibility and not to pass the buck back to him. We have been given the privilege of free will and God wants us to use that privilege constructively.

God wants us to work with him in healing the world's

ills. Some of these can be dealt with individually by us. (For instance, that poor, lonely old woman across the road. It is no use praying for someone else to go and visit her! We should be doing it.) Other and more difficult problems can only be dealt with collectively. And that is where prayer comes in.

I have compared prayer to a hammock. A hammock is something which is made up of a lot of pieces of string. Our little piece alone is nothing. Won't hold anyone up. But used with other pieces of string, it can support even a twenty-stone man!

Some people that we pray for can be helped by donations of money. (For example, the Leprosy Mission, to provide more doctors.) Millions of others are restored to health by doctors and nurses and it is only right that we shouid pray for them as well. Discovering new drugs is part of the healing process and so we should also pray for the scientists and chemists who do this vital work. There is no limit to the possibilities of prayer. Prayer is the raw material through which God makes things happen. If enough people pray for something, action will follow.

Unfortunately, people make too little use of prayer. They do not realize the value or the power of the gift that has been placed in their hands. Some people, sadly, still treat the sick list as a gossip column and speculate on what Mrs X has gone into hospital for this time. That is like using a bread van to carry manure.

If someone is in hospital, the first thing to do is to pray for him or her without speculating about their illness. It is enough to pray for "George". It would of course be helpful to know whether "George" is a baby or someone in a geriatric ward at Royal Victoria Hospital. If "George" is a baby then obviously we should also being praying for his parents in their anxiety. But if "George" is over 90 and suffering from double incontinence, we should be praying for a swift release from all his pain and humiliation.

Sometimes we have to pray for life. Sometimes for death. Different cases make for different prayers. Information does help us to pray more intelligently – but people's privacy has to be respected. The more we do know, the more directly we can target our prayers.

But, of course, our prayers are not always answered in the way we expect. We may pray for "George" to live – and he dies. Or, more embarrassingly, we pray for someone to die – and they live! This can be puzzling and painful. Although people still say we cannot buck "Fate" – that the date of our death is fixed . . . that God has planned it all – and (the splendid Dundee saying) "what's for you'll no go by you!" This is not the teaching of the Scottish Episcopal Church.

We believe that there is complete free will within the created order, with possibilities for good as well as for evil and that God permits this freedom. God does not plan our deaths. (I wouldn't plan anyone's death – and we can say for certain that God is a great deal more loving than David Shepherd!) Dying and living depends very much on the strength of our hearts and lungs. God is not all-powerful. Or perhaps we should say that, in this situation, he chooses not to exercise his full almighty power.

Therefore, when we hope or pray for someone to live, even after all our efforts and all God's efforts, he may still die. Equally, if we long for someone to have release in death, however much we may pray for an end to their suffering and however much God shares our longing, because of of a strong heart, our prayers may just not work. We have to pray as best we can and then accept the outcome. Just as we know God will do his best – and also have to accept the outcome. But this is no excuse for not praying.

It is important – especially for those who do not attend church regularly – to realize that we have a very special responsibility to care and pray for sick people. We do not live for ourselves. We live for others. And to neglect our prayers for people who are sick or in need is just as bad as the Levite and the priest who walked past on the other side. We must do our bit – in Church – and then at home. I *am* my brother's keeper – and so are you.

(September 1988)

Is Football A Religion?

As we approach the 1998 World Cup, we may be sure that every television channel and every newspaper in the country will devote immense amounts of time and space to covering this great international event. Thousands of supporters will troop across the Channel and millions more will be glued to their television sets for days on end. Hopes will soar; nerves will tingle. If we reach the final, the nation will be ecstatic; if we lose, there will be acute mental depression and deep heart-searching. Even if we do win, what do we get? An ugly piece of metal which was once described as "a pregnant angel doing deportment exercises with a wash-basin!" It is hard to believe that ordinary people can get so hyped up about a mere leather ball – but perhaps the truth is this: Football is no longer a game; it is a religion.

Even to the untutored eye, there is a lot about contemporary soccer that smacks of religion. There are parishes (local clubs), dioceses (leagues and divisions), and grand ecumenical occasions (friendlies)! Within each local church, there are clear lines of demarcation between priests and people. A north-end, south-end celebration with the holy-of-holies clearly marked out in green and white. No problem for the sanctuary boys knowing where they should be! The colour, of course, strictly Trinitarian!

We note that the disciples (or are they apostles?) are eleven in number, maintaining the ancient post-Good Friday line-out after Judas's betrayal. Instead of a wooden cross, they have a wooden E symbol (Easter with the "I" knocked out?) For Christians, there is the comforting presence of goal-nets reminding us that these players are still "fishers of men." Like the clergy in our own church, the disciples are decked out in fanciful liturgical vestments – shirts, shorts and boots.

At first, one might assume that they are celebrating the seasons of the Christian year. But no! They are merely tribal badges – like woad!

Instead of gongs and incense, we have rattles and whistles. Instead of the Toronto blessing, we have the Mexican wave. Instead of a bishop, we have a referee. Like his Episcopal counterpart, he is there to supervise the apostolic work of the players – to make sure they observe the strict canons of football lore – and book them (defrock them?) when they commit foul deeds. Like the bishop in the Christian Church, the referee is a controversial figure, especially when he intervenes too forcibly.

The new religion has its own special day for celebrating the sacred mysteries. Significantly, they have chosen Saturday – the day of the old Jewish Sabbath – for their principal service. But just as good Anglo-Catholics cannot do without a midweek celebration, so the soccer devotee must have his midweek celebration on Mondays or Wednesdays – not forgetting the blissful joys of the UEFA Cup which may rejoice the hearts of the faithful.

As with the Christian Church, there are notable places of pilgrimage. Not exactly Lourdes, Canterbury or Walsingham – but Tannadice, Hampden or Wembley. Every week, coaches filled with the sick and anxious, the lonely and the unloved, take them to these well-known centres of spiritual refreshment. Clad in home-made stoles, clutching their sacramental drink (McEwans or something a little stronger), waving their baptismal rattles, singing their deeply-felt hymns and chants, they descend on the life-giving turf for a mere touch at the hem of the garments of these apostles.

For these are no ordinary men. They are saints – martyrs – clad in shining white apparel – the beaming, blessed ones whom faithful souls long to see. Their Communion of Saints is rich in heroes. St Edward of Sheringham; the inimitable Paul of Gazza and Blessed Kevin-ever-Keegan. They have fought the fight; they have run the race; they have entered the celestial pantheon to which all great players go.

On the pitch, there is more joy over one shot that brings salvation, than over ninety-and-nine good passes which excite no enthusiasm. There is the kiss of peace, constantly exchanged between ecstatic worshippers. There is the grovelling in the mud for repentance (presumably a latter day version of sackcloth and ashes?)

There is vicious conflict between rival clubs – so closely paralleling the hostility between the different churches that it is difficult to see the difference between Catholics and Protestants, Rangers and Celtic. In the ecclesiastical armoury, there is one ultimate weapon – excommunication. In football, it is called relegation. In both religions, the ultimate weapon is used sparingly.

Then we might note the male chauvinist domination of the sport. (Surely this must be a fitting subject for the Sex Discrimination Act?) Why are there no women priests on the field? Is a woman congenitally unfit to touch the sacred mysteries of ball and whistle? Is it because the Great Footballer-up-above is male and plays for Elysium Athletic? Who knows?

For those unfitted by age or ordination to pass beyond the altar rails and enter the sacred pitch, there is some minor compensation. Not exactly the River Jordan or Lake Galilee . . . But for the faithful worshipper, pools are provided weekly into which he may dip the tip of his finger or the note in his pocket. For some, these pools have wrought stupendous miracles – huge cheques; but for others, there has been sorrowful disillusion. They may never live to enter the Promised Land; their god may have failed; but they are frightened to stop. This may be the Big 'Un! "Onward football players . . . "

We are told it is only a game . . . something essentially simple like ludo or hopscotch, which has been elaborated and commercialized out of all recognition. As St Paul is to Jesus, so is modern football to the game we used to play. Fathers in the congregation drag their sons away from the Christian Church and offer their virile offspring on the altar of this pagan deity, thinking they are doing something good for their children. But what about the tribal violence, the torn cartilages or the fractured skulls? The foul language, the violence on the terraces? Would not an hour a week at Sunday School do them more good?

The question is: "Does it work?" Does this new religion

bring life or resurrection to its supporters? Or is it merely bread and circuses – a palliative to fill up the emptiness of our everyday lives? If it didn't exist, what on earth would we watch on TV? Snooker, rugby, tennis – more little balls being knocked about? Lenin once said that religion was the opium of the people. And he was right. But the question is – which of the two is the opium which dulls our senses, drugs the population and provides an escape from reality? Is it Christianity – or football? Before the shrine of the impending World Cup, perhaps our Lady of Fatima will give us the answer!

(March 1998)

The Courage To Let Go

Having spoken to many people over recent months, I was surprised to find how many of them were in favour of euthanasia. The discussions were of course sparked off by the case of Anthony Bland, the young football fan, who was so badly injured in the Hillsborough disaster that he has been in a permanent vegetative state for the past three years.

Talking about the case has encouraged many people to say what they would do in similar circumstances. And they have no doubt what they would wish for themselves – and for their loved ones. A quick and peaceful end. For them as much as for their families.

We do it for animals – but not for human beings. The medical profession is governed by the Hippocratic oath to preserve life at all costs. And when a doctor does not do this – as we have again seen recently – he is branded as a murderer even when he has brought to an end the sufferings of a patient who was terminally ill on what could only be the most compassionate of grounds.

The medical profession struggles so hard to keep people alive that I often wonder whether they believe in eternal life? If they believed that people would be happier on the other side of death – why delay? Do they think the death of a patient is a sign of failure?

What should be our Christian attitude to euthanasia? Should we stick to the letter of the law – or should we take the law into our own hands in the name of compassion and mercy?

Regrettably, the Bible gives us no clear answer to this moral dilemma. Jesus spent much of his ministry healing the sick and occasionally raising the dead. The age in which he lived was a very violent age when many people died young. To survive to a ripe old age was considered something of a miracle. Even as a sign of divine favour. Old age was respected. And during the last 2000 years, Christianity has always been in the forefront of those wishing to preserve and prolong life and to assist people who are dying to be given all the care and attention they need.

One only has to look at Mother Teresa's work for people dying on the streets of Calcutta. The way she and her sisters gather up the broken bones of humanity, look after them in their hospice, wash them, clothe them, care for them with love till they die. That is certainly Christianity in one of its most dramatic and appealing forms.

In our country, such things are in the hands of doctors, nurses and hospital administrators. They do all they can to enable people to die decently and with dignity. But the question arises: "When is it right to let a person die?" Should the last moment be prolonged as long as possible?

I find it very odd that at one end of our hospitals, we find doctors and nurses agonizing about whether the 88

45

year old Mrs Smith should be allowed to die whilst, at the other end of the hospital, they are busy aborting one foetus every fifteen minutes – without the slightest scruple.

Since the Abortion Act of 1967, they have had complete immunity under the law. They are permitted to destroy a foetus which is capable of growing into a complete human being with all its life before it. I find in this a terrible hypocrisy. That the medical profession will struggle to maintain life at one end – when it is scarcely worth preserving; and yet terminate a life full of potential and growth at the other.

To me it seems that we have got things completely the wrong way round. The foetus should be allowed to live; the terminally ill patient should be allowed to die. On a day of their own choosing or on a day when family and doctors agree enough is enough.

It is high time the Church gave a lead in such ethical matters. We are always to be seen skulking round in the background, biting our fingernails, waiting for others to take these vital decisions. If we wait for guidance from our bishops, nothing will ever be done. They have the moral courage of wood lice. We should decide what Life is . . . and what it is not. These are my views:

Life is about a functioning organism. Life is about growing and developing – in body and mind. Life is about relationships with other people. Life is physical but also spiritual. We are body as well as spirit. When a body becomes no more than an outer shell . . . When a body ceases to function without mechanical help . . . When a body is clearly in terminal decay . . . When a person is incapable of sustaining a relationship with other people, then earthly life is over. We should have the courage of our beliefs to let go; to commend the spirit of that person into the hands of a loving Father. To turn off the switch on the side of the machine; to cease prolonging earthly existence and enable the person to enter into that spiritual world which is richer and brighter than anything we can imagine.

Terminating a life is an act of compassion. It is an act of faith in the kingdom of God which lies beyond. Life itself does not end – because the spirit of a man or woman goes on for ever. Terminating an earthly existence which is already over is an act of liberation. Liberating the spirit. Death has to come to all of us one day. When that moment draws near, we have to have the courage to say: "Yes" – not because we are callous or inhuman. But because we believe firmly that Life goes on.

We do it for animals. Surely we deserve equal – if not better – treatment? This is the gut instinct of ordinary people. Having sat at the bedside of numerous dying people and sharing the misery of their friends and family in that long ordeal, I think the time has come to ask our legislators and the medical profession not to drag out the agony of dying; but to have the courage to let go.

(22nd November 1992)

Ambassadors For Christ

A few weeks ago – quite by surprise – I found myself being introduced to members of the PLO delegation which was visiting Dundee. Now the Palestine Liberation Organization is one of my least favourite organizations. Like the IRA, it has brought immense unhappiness and misery to many thousands of people. Its policy of bombing, murder and holding children hostage at gunpoint has given it wide publicity. But, in the process, it has – again like the IRA – aroused the hostility of most civilized people, who doubt whether an organization which lives and fights in such an unprincipled and murderous way is worth talking to.

What then was my reaction to these delegates from the PLO? Should I shake their hands? Or should I turn on my heel and walk away? Should I tell them what I thought of their hideous policy? Or should I welcome them as strangers and listen to what they had to say? You may be sure I had a very difficult ten seconds, trying to make up my mind.

And I have to say this. They were very nice people. They were polite. They had a good sense of humour. They were open, friendly and talkative. They believed in the justice of their cause. And, without pushing too hard, they wanted British people to share their feelings and understand the plight of the Palestinian people.

Although my feelings about the PLO did not change one iota, I could not help thinking what excellent ambassadors these men were for their cause. They did not come brandishing weapons. They came with a smile and soft words. And, if one knew nothing about the history of the Middle East during these past few years, it would have been very easy to swallow their propaganda – because they were such nice people.

And I thought to myself, what a contrast there was between the Church and the PLO. Here is an organization which sponsors violence and murder – represented by what appeared to be good and sincere men. Whilst the Church, which is supposed to be a vessel of grace, peace and love, so often makes a very poor showing. Its representatives scowl at the world. They scowl at each other. They quarrel. They are divided into factions. Within parishes, all we hear about are fights and disagreements over petty matters such as candles or vestments.

The Church has been around for 2000 years – but it has not changed. In his second letter to the Christians at Corinth, St Paul urged his readers to become "ambassadors for Christ." One can imagine the Corinthians pausing at this point; looking at each other with some uncertainty; reaching for their dictionaries! Saying to each other: "What is an ambassador?" We might very well ask the same question.

An ambassador represents his country abroad. If you

go to the right part of London, you will find a bewildering array of embassies belonging to Spain, Bulgaria, Greece and dozens more. The ambassador from Spain is there to make sure that the feelings and decisions of the Spanish government are known to the British government. He is there to convey the opinions and decisions of the British government to his people in Madrid. He is there to protect Spanish citizens whilst they are here in the United Kingdom. And, being a diplomat, he is required to maintain very high standards of behaviour because he is representing his King – or his President – here.

We find ourselves in the same position. Once again, there are two countries involved. There is the Kingdom of God (or the Kingdom of Heaven, as Jesus called it) and the Kingdom of Men. One is a world of God's creation where his rules have the force of law; the other is a sort of jungle where the heavenly commandments are barely perceived and where people very often live their lives in complete opposition to God. And God has chosen us to represent him here. As Christians, we belong to his world; but by virtue of our homes and jobs, we live in a Kingdom where God's laws are constantly disobeyed.

Now, the first necessity in this situation is to provide information. People need to be told about this other Kingdom. If we don't tell them, they will never know anything about the Kingdom of God. With perhaps a million active Christians in Britain – hopefully more – there should be no problem getting the message across.

But if we say nothing, we cannot blame the natives for their ignorance. If they reject our message and declare it to be stupid or untrue; this does not mean the Christian message is stupid and untrue. It means that we have not presented it as clearly as we should.

It may be that having looked at our behaviour as Christian people, the natives may have said to themselves: "Whatever their beliefs, these Christians do not seem to practice what they preach! They talk about love and forgiveness; but we don't see much of that in their dealings with other people. There is a fatal inconsistency between what they say and what they do."

Like the Spanish ambassador, whose job it is to protect the lives of Spanish citizens who are in Britain, it is also our job to protect the lives and interests of our fellow citizens. Now this raises an interesting point. God reckons that everyone in this world belongs to his Kingdom. God reckons that the whole world belongs to him. He is not just interested in Christians but with everything that lives and moves on this planet. Therefore, as Christians, we have to care about the poor, the hungry and the unemployed. What happens to a small child in a shanty town in South America matters very much to God. It should therefore matter a great deal to us.

Thirdly, as I have said, the Ambassador is there to represent the views of the British people to his own government. It is our duty to represent the needs of the world to God. To appeal to him for help and assistance wherever we see a genuine need. As Christians, we do not live with our heads in the clouds; we live very much down here. We are intercessors for our fellow human beings. This is a vital role.

We seek to bring all the power of God to bear on human sickness and sin. To put him to the test. Jesus said that, whatever we ask in his Name, he will do it. Well, if we are to have any credibility in this world, people must not just hear our message but also see the Kingdom of God in action.

The Ambassador's job is often a lonely one. He is in the minority. Christians have always been in the minority. Active Christians an even smaller minority. But people who believe in something will always change the world for the better. William Wilberforce ended slavery after a very personal campaign against massive odds and enormous vested interests. Florence Nightingale changed the face of medicine and nursing care almost single-handedly. In our own time, Mother Teresa has devoted her life to caring for the sick and the dying in the streets of Calcutta and her example and her faith have been an encouragement to us all. And yet she started with less than five rupees in her pocket.

In the Early Church, people could see other people being healed; sins being forgiven. There was a love and a joy about the Christian community that was infectious. They seemed to be such good people, that outsiders wanted to join them. And there were no barriers. It seemed that "in heaven, there was an open door." Immigrants welcome! No trouble about visas!

Last week, I was visiting a Vestry in this city (which shall be nameless) trying to encourage that congregation to grow. And I was talking about going round, banging on doors, showing a face. And one lady said to me: "Do you think that is the best way to find Episcopalians?" And I said to her: "We're not just looking for Episcopalians. We're looking for any of God's people! We're trying to bring his light to shine on them; to bring them home; to bind up their wounds; to provide them with an anchor in this restless, turbulent world."

(People think so much about badges and denominations. But we are roving ambassadors for Jesus Christ; trying to make his name known; to show his love and care; and to welcome people into the fellowship of his Church.)

I remember that the lady looked a little surprised. She didn't see herself as an ambassadress. She didn't think she was representing anyone. She didn't realize there was a need to go out looking for lost sheep. She didn't realize that the extension of Christ's Kingdom depended on her. But it does.

Now one may not think much of the calibre of the ambassadors God has chosen. It is a pretty motley crew. But, of course, it always was. St Peter made lots of mistakes. He wouldn't even eat with Gentile Christians till St Paul told him he was wrong. There has always been an unwillingness amongst Christians to open their mouths; to talk to people; to seem enthusiastic about the Christian faith. If we were travel agents selling holidays to a foreign country, no one would ever want to go there!

We must beef up our presentation. We must do more to encourage each other. Above all, we must recognize that whether we are Catholics, Episcopalians or Church of Scotland, we are all ambassadors of the same Kingdom. Of the same King. We shall serve him much better if we work together. If we make ourselves presentable. If our message is carefully thought-out. Well-presented.

We have a Gospel to proclaim – a Gospel that is true. A

Gospel which has everything to offer to the citizens of this world. A healing. A caring. A peace of God. A message of hope, which needs to be heard. And we should not be afraid to present that message with great joy and enthusiasm. Our faith will nourish faith.

But our faith needs to be wholly sincere and genuine. Because we are ambassadors – not for the PLO or the IRA – but Ambassadors for God himself! What a privilege! What a challenge!

(28th June 1981)

Judge Or Baby?

This is the time of year when balance sheets are drawn up in preparation for the Church's AGM. Every penny spent is analyzed by an independent examiner under the terms of the Charities' Commission. Questions are asked. Who was the money paid to? Why was there no receipt?

These are difficult moments for a Church treasurer. Twelve months on, it is difficult to remember why this or that was done. It is rather like going into a confessional box to admit to sins we had quite forgotten! And then, of course, the treasurer has to face the Vestry, the congregation and, perhaps, an Inland Revenue inspector.

It is interesting that we audit our finances so carefully, but we completely fail to audit our spiritual lives . . . They do not seem to have an equal importance . . . We may have done some terrible things during the past year; but who is going to call us to account? In fact, we may have done absolutely nothing for God; but who will ever know?

As we come to the end of another year in the life of the Church, we can be certain that no one will put our faith, our love, our ministry under a microscope. No one will ever publish our spiritual balance sheet (thank God!). No one will ever know . . .

Well, that is what we would like to think. But God is not blind. He sees . . . He knows . . . And, as our Gospel reminds us this morning, there is judgement. There is a day of reckoning. But what is at issue is not our finances; but our individual behaviour as human beings. We shall not be judged on complicated theological issues – or even our knowledge of the Bible; but on how we have treated Mr Brown and Mrs Smith. This is rather frightening! Because we probably don't like Mrs Smith; and Mr Brown . . . well, Mr Brown has a stutter and takes a long time to express himself; and rather than waste time, we avoid him. And yet, horror of horrors, we suddenly realize that it is how we treat these ordinary folk, that will determine our final destiny.

As we come up to Christmas, we are happy to welcome Jesus as a baby – weak, defenceless, vulnerable. Someone who wouldn't say "boo" to a goose! Nothing threatening about a baby. But it is much less acceptable to meet Jesus as our Judge. Unfortunately, that is one of the unpleasant realities of the New Testament. Whenever people met Jesus, there was always judgement. The poor old Pharisees thought they had everything taped. Till they met Jesus. When they met him, he questioned everything they did. Meeting Jesus exposed them as liars, hypocrites – and even worse – murderers. Every encounter with Jesus was an act of judgement – even for Pontius Pilate. They thought they were judging him; but it was the other way round.

There is a famous story of an American tourist who was visiting the Uffizi gallery in Florence. As she left, she said to the curator: "I didn't think much of the pictures."

To which, he replied: "Madam, it is not the pictures which are being judged!"

In our Gospel for this morning (St Matthew 25 vv 31 – 46 – read it!) we have the classic excuse: "Lord, we never knew!" Eighty million Germans swore blind: "We never knew anything about the extermination of the Jews." "It came as a complete surprise." "We never did anything."

But that was the point. Faced with an issue of simple humanity, they did nothing. Here in Dundee, we know, thousands of abortions have taken place. We know that many of them are babies with a chance of life. But their lives are terminated unnaturally – every day. We may say: "Blame the doctors! Don't blame us!" It is a moral issue. And we do nothing. Foxhunting? Yes, we are happy to ban it. But aborting babies? No.

God does not judge us on things outside our control. But he does judge us on the ordinary things within our grasp. The simple humanity we show – or don't show – towards others. So judgement is not tomorrow. It is today. By our actions; by our words; by our silence – we may be condemning others. But we are also condemning ourselves.

I know that this is not a cheerful message – for any of us. And I know that, as a clergyman, I shall be judged more harshly than you. We do not like being looked at all that closely. We admit to being neither black nor white – but rather grey. We live in a country where the Government would like to see everyone having a chance of going to University. In the same spirit of tolerance and charity, we assume that everyone – however sinful – will have their place in heaven.

Not so! We are not being judged by the standards of New Labour or the Welfare state – but by One who has experienced our inhumanity at first hand. Who knows our weaknesses and strengths. He asks us directly: "Could we not have shown more compassion? Could we not have said something comforting? Was there nothing we could have done to help that poor person? Did we have to bear all those grudges year after year?"

Our behaviour towards other people does matter. It may not seem to matter much down here. But when we encounter Jesus – as we all shall do – it will become a matter of blinding importance. It will be no use saying: "I never knew." Of course we knew! It is far worse than £10,000 missing from the balance sheet. The things we have failed to do.

Because – as Jesus said – it is how we treat one of his brothers and sisters – the little people – the despised people – the uncomfortable, difficult people – that ultimately matters. If we have no love in our hearts – and no forgiveness, then the message is quite clear. We shall be judged.

And we shall have no one to blame but ourselves. We may turn our backs on the baby Jesus at Christmas, but we will not escape him as our Judge.

Fortunately, there is still time to change.

(24th November 2002)

It Pays To Advertise

There is a popular saying: "It pays to advertise" – and in my experience, it is true. If you want people to come to some public entertainment, there is nothing better than a well-placed advertisement which catches the eye. Even our Church Christmas card is a sort of advertisement for our Christmas services. It says: "This is what is happening. Come and join us!"

The trouble is that God himself does not like advertising. That is why Jesus did so much of his preaching in parables. So that "seeing they might not see; and hearing they might not understand!" What a curious idea! The very opposite of good advertising practice where the principal object is to let people see your product.

See it so much, they want it. Want it so much that they cannot live without it. The object of all propaganda is to get your message across – so that people do understand. So that they will buy.

But secrecy has always been God's policy. He prefers to keep in the background. To appear – in the Old Testament – in a pillar of fire or cloud. He refused to show himself to Moses. He spoke through the prophets. He intervened indirectly. The majority of people did not know what God was up to. They did not know what had happened till later – until they were able to piece the evidence together. Like Jacob, they said: "Truly the Lord was in this place and we just didn't know it."

And this is particularly true of the birth in Bethlehem that first Christmas. No one knew what was happening. Even Mary and Joseph were somewhat confused about what God had planned. Jesus was born as a stranger . . . as an outcast . . . in a stable. No one was prepared for his arrival. There was no bed. No warmth. The simple human drama in Bethlehem passed the world by. "Lord, when did we see you a stranger and welcome you?" Nobody told us.

Only to a few shepherds and a trio of wise men did God lift a corner of the veil to show what he was up to. But why choose them? It's all very odd. Even when St Matthew and St Luke wrote up the story of the birth in Bethlehem, they failed to realize the main point behind the Incarnation. It took St John to really explain the mystery: "The Word was made flesh and dwelt amongst us . . . " It wasn't an ordinary birth. It was the most extraordinary act in all creation. That God was in Jesus being born physically into a world He had created. Nothing like it had ever happened before. It will never happen again. And nobody important was there! No reporters! No officials!

So God does not advertise his deeds. He prefers to act secretly. So that we hardly know what is happening. If we want to see God at work, we have to look in some very dark corners – like Calcutta – to see what is going on. The facts will not be presented to us on a plate. We may choose to ignore the birth of a baby in Bethlehem. We may say it is irrelevant to our modern life. But in turning our backs, we shall be making the biggest mistake in our lives.

Because only part of our lives are lived out down here. This is only a time of preparation for the full life – the eternal life – which we shall enjoy in heaven. God wants to establish a relationship with us in this life before we come to the glories of his Kingdom. He wants us to know him, to understand him, to worship him, to work with him in this life. To continue his work of praying for – and healing – the miseries of this world. To be his friends and disciples – now! To understand his mysteries. To enjoy his presence in the sacraments. To let him dwell in us.

And the way into all this – is understanding what God was actually doing that first Christmas. God being born into our world. Sharing our sorrows. Knowing our difficulties. Knowing himself what it means to be human.

Christmas is about God. To think it is about Santa Claus or stockings or booze or turkeys is a great mistake. We are not worshipping a dead turkey. We are not worshipping an imaginary saviour coming down a chimney in an all-electric house.

There is only one present this Christmastide. And that is the infant Jesus. The only gift. The greatest gift. The gift which, if taken into the hearts of men and women, will bring peace to our war-torn world.

Because if we really take Christmas and what it means into our hearts, we cannot kill people – or hurt them. The love of God would shine through us. If everyone could begin to accept this gift, imagine what changes would follow! If everyone began to see themselves and others as the children of God. If the love of God flowed freely . . . what a blessing for mankind!

The world prefers all the glamour and glitter of a commercial Christmas. A false god and no mistake! People respond to all the advertising – all the gimmicks. They go mad spending . . . spending . . . spending. And for what? Today's turkey is tomorrow's indigestion. Today's beautifully wrapped present is tomorrow's waste paper in the dustbin. The fine bottle of claret goes down the pan on its way to the sewage plant. The cards are torn up on the twelfth day. Nothing lasts. Soon it is all gone. And after Christmas, as we go back to work, people say: "Did you have a nice Christmas?" And we say; "Yes" because we do not like to admit we have been conned.

So then, what does God offer us this Christmas? What shall we find when we come into his presence? If we listen to the words of the angels? As we sing our carols and meditate upon the message of that first Christmas?

First of all, it will cost you very little – perhaps nothing at all. You can come into the Church and worship God for free. You can receive his eternal gifts in the bread and wine at Communion. You can come as close to God as it is humanly possible to do so. And the glory and joy of Christmas will radiate through your mind, your heart, your life.

The brightness of Christmas is not to be found in the shop windows or on TV. There is no show in Bethlehem. There is only the real thing. And those who come close to Jesus at the Eucharist will find him – the real Christmas gift.

"No ear may hear his coming;
But in this world of sin
Where meek souls will receive him still,
The *real* Christ enters in."
May I wish you all a happy and holy Christmas.

(Christmas Day 1980)

Amazing Grace

For most Christian people, the greatest spiritual thrill at Christmas-time is to hear the opening words of St John's Gospel, read at a Carol Service or the Midnight Eucharist. Everything builds up to this great literary climax. We may sit whilst we hear the story of the shepherds, the angels or the stable . . . but we stand for St John. We listen to every single word as the evangelist explains the great cosmic truths which lie behind the simple birth at Bethlehem:

"In the beginning, was the Word . . . "

We are so used to hearing these familiar words that we perhaps fail to realize the brilliant way St John has managed to combine traditional Jewish theology with the latest Greek philosophy – in a mere six words.

To any Jew, the first three words: "In the beginning . . ." would have conjured up the first chapter of the book of Genesis – the story of God's creation of the heaven and the earth. But the concept of "the Word" embraced all that the Greeks understood about Life, Energy, Power, Reason – even Wisdom itself. Everything that is involved in making things move, act, think or be – was summed up in "the Word."

And St John hammers home his point: "The Word was with God . . . and the Word was God." So far, so good. No one could disagree. St John speaks of God's creative power: "All things were made by him . . . " He says that God has given us life. And this God-given life is something that really shines out in the darkness of this world. An eternal life – an eternal Light – which cannot be extinguished or overcome by anything else in this world.

Unfortunately, he says, powerful though this life is – and however bright the Light – people just did not seem to understand where it all came from and what it was all for. Two thousand years of Jewish history hadn't really changed the Jews. They didn't seem to understand God or his purpose any better than anyone else. Even the ultra-civilized Greeks and Romans still worshipped bits of wood and stone. They cut up wild birds and examined their entrails – expecting that these disgusting objects might tell them something they didn't know. People remained completely ignorant of their Creator. Even those who might have expected to be closest to the truth were blind, deaf and cold. God was still a perfect stranger.

Greeks and Jews would have nodded their heads in agreement. The Deity was certainly very mysterious. So how could God make himself known? Verse 14 is the key verse. The one we know so well. But, imagine you were reading it for the first time:

"The Word became flesh and dwelt amongst us."

This was quite revolutionary. Not to say a total impossibility – to both Jews and Greeks. It was all very well God being God. But how could God not be God?

The word: "flesh" for a Greek, summed up the totality of human life. Human nature, a human body, a perishable object capable of sin and mess. But "the Word" was something abstract and divine. It was outwith – above – transcendent – ethereal.

"The Word" becoming flesh was a contradiction in terms. As if you might say: "Space is mud. Or, air is concrete. Or, good is bad." It would require a considerable leap of the imagination – a considerable confounding of logic – for either a Jew or Greek to see how the invisible Deity could be born "in the flesh." The idea was unthinkable.

But St John says: "It's happened! We've seen it. We've touched it. It's real." Grace and truth have come to us in this person – Jesus Christ. And through him, we have all received the fullness of divine life. His love was shed abroad in our hearts. His Spirit is a gift that dwells within us. None of us have ever seen God at any time – but through this Man, God has made himself known to us once and for all.

This is the substance of St John's message. He is not concerned with a little miracle down at the pub in Bethlehem. He is overwhelmed by the earth-shaking consequences of God's action in human history. The Incarnation; the Crucifixion; the Resurrection. The whole life of this Man. Light has shined in the darkness. A blinding, glorious Light, revealing all the love, the power and the majesty of God. His life pouring out in us. Making us the children of God.

Can you see why St John did not waste his time talking about donkeys, stars or shepherds? He is not interested in a mere Nativity! A Christmas card picture – however pretty. He is staggered by the immensity of the Divine Creator bursting right into our world – into our life. Making himself known to mortal men and women "in the flesh." All the other Gospel writers realized this. But only St John, in these brilliant eighteen verses, was able to express the immensity of Divine power revealed in Jesus.

St John doesn't say to us: "Now, come on, you chaps, do you believe in the virgin conception?" "Do you really believe there were three wise men and a star?" He says: "Don't just look at the packaging! Look at the inner reality!" This is God in action. Not a fairy story for adults. This is the God who created all this vast world. This unknown God doing something quite unbelievable; something quite wonderful for us.

This is what we are celebrating at Christmas time. The glorious God of heaven coming to us – in the flesh. In a recognizable form. An ordinary human life which encompasses birth, death and resurrection. This is something so totally unexpected, that it changes our whole attitude to life, to God, to other people. Now we can have some idea of what God is like. Not a cold, remote figure, who treats us like puppets. Not a cosmic sadist who rains down fire and brimstone on unrepentant sinners. But a warm, friendly Father-figure whom we can approach. Who understands our problems, our sorrows and our joys because he has experienced them himself. This is the greatest thing that has ever happened in human history.

But the trouble is – even despite St John's splendid Gospel – people still do not see what Christmas is all about. "It's all about families," we are told. "It's all about children . . . food . . . drink . . . enjoying yourself." But it isn't. Christmas is all about God.

And until people have discovered what it is all about – until they have received the real gift which is being offered – both the Church and the world will continue to be very sad and unhappy places. We shall remain in darkness – despite the Light of Christ. And the real Christmas will pass us by.

So then, St John's Gospel is not just beautiful language; magic prose; it is not just poetry. It expresses simply – but gloriously – the very essence of life itself. The greatest fact ever revealed. The truth about God. His life with us.

Today, as we reach the last day of Christmas, before we finally shut up shop and take down our tree, we have a final glimpse of the glory of heaven. A fleeting chance to hear the message of the angels before they pass back into heaven:

"Glory to God in the highest,
And on earth, peace and goodwill unto men."

(5th January 1997)

A Gift For Life

Only two weeks have passed since the great Festival of Christmas, but I imagine that – even now – you may have some difficulty remembering who gave you what gift. I usually keep a list so that I can remember whom I have to thank for all the bottles of wine and other useful gifts I have received. Without that list, I should be lost.

But there was one Christmas when the gifts were not forgotten. Gifts that are remembered by even the most sceptic agnostic . . . the most diehard atheist. The gifts of the wise men – gold, frankincense and myrrh. Such strange gifts to give to a baby! Surely a rattle, a woolly animal or a box of bricks might have been more appropriate?

Perhaps even the wise men themselves had doubts. Gifts which would have seemed appropriate at a royal court looked quite out of place in a small hovel in Bethlehem. They probably felt disappointed. A sense of anti-climax. It was not what they had expected. They probably felt that expensive gifts were wasted on people like that. I imagine they went home deflated, disillusioned, never realizing that their gifts would always be remembered . . . for their symbolic value in the life of

Christ. Gold for a king; frankincense for a priest; myrrh for immortality. In those gifts was encapsulated the life of Jesus.

Very often, the gifts we receive, shape our lives. You may recollect that at a very dismal moment in the life of Winston Churchill, his wife went out a bought him a box of paints. Churchill would always have been remembered as a writer and politician; but to his life was added a new dimension – a non-competitive, silent gift which brought him great solace and comfort – and, of course, great pleasure – for the next forty years.

Similarly, Agatha Christie's mother noticed that, when her daughter had flu, she was bored and restless – couldn't be bothered to read anything. Her mother handed her a notebook and pen and said: "Why don't you write a story yourself?"

I am sure that many of you have had the experience of receiving a gift which has launched you into some major interest in life. A piece of jewellery. A book. A stamp album. Perhaps a set of golf clubs. A packet of seeds. Something which has had a profound influence on your life. These things seem to come out of the blue. Almost by accident. The Bible says that all good gifts come from above; and the poet, Robert Browning, says that God's gifts put man's best dreams to shame.

Perhaps they are not just accidents. Perhaps those who give us good things are guided – as the wise men were – but not by a star. St Paul, in his letter to the Corinthians, points out that we all have an immense variety of gifts. Some great, some small; but all of them very precious.

Each one has a vital part to play in our lives. Each one

makes its own particular contribution to the development of the whole person. I have often found that even in the smallest Christian community in the Diocese, there are always people with the vital gifts which the community needs. They are there – just where they are needed.

It cannot be an accident. The Church should be in the business of helping people to develop those gifts and use them – not just for the benefit of the Church, but also the wider community.

I remember, a few years ago, organizing a Diocesan Conference on the subject of healing. We invited a very devout man from the Guild of Health; but I also invited a professional faith healer – by way of contrast. The man from the Guild of Health spoke very beautifully but the faith healer immediately invited the audience to try an experiment to see if any of them had a gift for healing. Each person had to lay their hands on their neighbour's back. Did they feel anything? Was there any sensation?

Some people got terribly excited. Others felt absolutely nothing. But, from the Conference, people came away realizing that the gift of healing might be something which they had – something they could share and use for the benefit of other people.

As we heard in this morning's Gospel, Jesus was chiefly noted for his gifts of healing. It may have been something he was born with – but it was not something he used till after his thirtieth birthday. He too was regarded as something of a fraud. The Pharisees thought he carried out his miracles with the power of Beelzebub. But it was a gift which he exercised right to the end – even in the garden of Gethsemane, when he healed the wounded servant's ear.

The best gifts do not come ready-made. We have to work on them. A set of golf clubs will not make you a Seve Ballesteros – or a Tiger Woods. A book of music will not make you a great opera singer. The skills have to be developed – tried out over a period of years – before one has any hope of achieving perfection.

The hard thing about receiving gifts is that some people seem to fare better than others. I am sure we have all known Christmases when other people have got things that we should have liked – whilst we had to make do with things that were boring and ordinary. (Another pair of gloves!) Perhaps we feel bitter that we have been dealt such a poor hand. It makes us jealous of the success of others.

But as St Paul tries to tell us, everyone's gifts are equally important. The widow's mite is just as important as the £1000 cheque. We may say a bigger thank you for the cheque; but the widow's mite is not to be scorned; because it probably represents an even greater sacrifice on the part of the giver.

The gift tells us something about the person who gives it. How they see us. I often wonder why people give me so many bottles at Christmas. Do they think I am a secret alcoholic? And how we receive the gift – how we use it – tells us something about ourselves. No one who gives a gift expects it to be put away in a cupboard – or thrown into the dustbin – and never used.

The gifts we receive are meant to be used. They should enrich our lives – and bring us joy. Perhaps they may also improve the lives of other people. My gifts of wine are not meant to be scoffed greedily in some dark corner of the Rectory. They are there to be shared. All the cash gifts that I received at Christmas have been put into buying new anthem books for the choir. It is something which gives me the greatest pleasure. I hope they will prove very useful; and that we shall all benefit from the beautiful music which will be outpoured.

That is the message of Epiphany. To offer our gifts – however strange – however simple those gifts are. To see them used by God – and by other people. So that the world may be a brighter, richer place – for everyone.

The greatest enemy for any Christian is "self"- centring everything on "me". Taking everything in; giving nothing out. That is sin. The great thing about Epiphany is giving our treasures away; sharing them with others. Surprisingly, giving brings us greater happiness than receiving.

And what is true for us is equally true of God. He gave us his Son. We, in return, offer him our gifts – time, talents, skills, love. We may not understand the significance of the gifts we offer. They may not seem important enough – good enough. Others can offer more spectacular gifts. But in the life of the Church – in the life of the world – they will be just what is needed. Gold, frankincense and myrrh. Perhaps. But also the treasures of our hearts – the greatest gifts of all.

(10th January 1999)

It's All In The Mind

Anyone who has tried to give up smoking . . . to refuse an extra drink at a party . . . to compulsively buy some extravagant item of clothing . . . to share some juicy piece of gossip . . . to start revising for a forthcoming examination on a warm summer's day when there are better things to do . . . knows what temptation means.

There are forces at work undermining us. An overpowering craving. A willingness to surrender. A total loss of self-control. Acute laziness in the face of duty. We give way. We want to give way! We will give way time and again. We will never stop giving in to temptation. Even St Paul bewailed his own personal failings: "The good that I would, I do not; but the evil I would not, I do."

In the old days, people talked about the battle between the flesh and the spirit. All the bad things were blamed on "the sins of the flesh." It was our animal nature, they said. But they were wrong. The flesh is completely neutral. The trouble is always in the mind.

The mind is a very dangerous place. You can look at the outward face of a person and never imagine the fires that burn within. The outer respectability . . . the inner lusts. The responsible human being . . . and the coward that lurks just under the surface. Your temptations are not mine. I have no desire to smoke even one cigarette; but I may be power hungry! You may be consumed with greed; she may be jealous. But all these unpleasant features are, so to speak, under the bonnet. Not immediately apparent.

When Jesus taught his disciples to pray: "Lead us not into temptation . . . " he knew that the real sins only begin when we have given way. Once we have decided – in our mind's eye – that the apple looks good to eat . . . that it cannot possibly do us any harm . . . why shouldn't we have it . . . who can stop us anyway? And, afterwards: "Well, it didn't do us any harm, did it?" The slow, insidious descent down the hill of permissiveness into real sin.

Of course, it didn't matter that Adam ate an apple! It was only one apple. Nothing to make a great fuss about. It didn't hurt anyone else. Saying that he couldn't eat it was a ridiculous rule! An infringement of his civil liberties! No one would notice what he did. A quick bite . . .

But this act of disobedience was what St Paul called "the sin of Adam." The mental struggle which we lose. The battle between conscience and our own selfish desires. Conscience says one thing; instinct does another. Because of our natural human weakness we inevitably give way. The deed is done; and the way is open to do it again. And again – and again – and again.

Whether one agrees with the Roman Catholic Church or not, the sacramental act of confession – so often cruelly mocked in comedy programmes – does provide an opportunity when people can confront their most besetting sins; and perhaps do something about them.

The trouble with temptation is that we so often deny – even to ourselves – that there is any problem at all.

We can cope. We can resist – if we want to. There is a point beyond which we will not go. There are some things we would never say. Some things we would never do. And then, we do them! We say them! We go beyond our own self-appointed limits. We realize the battle is already lost. We need help – professional help – to overcome our sins.

So then, the mind is a battlefield. All sorts of mental struggles are going on in there every day. Battles between right and wrong. Indulgence versus self-control. Which one will win? In your heart of hearts, you know the answer. Every time, it will be the good, the prudent, the sensible, the wholesome – which bites the dust.

Logic suggests that the quicker we come to terms with temptation, the better chance there is of winning. It is easier to stop smoking when you are on five a day than when you are on twenty. It is better to stop after the first glass of wine than after No.5. It would be preferable not to go into that shop in the first place; once you are at the counter, it is too late. It is probably better to stop after the first dirty joke rather than endure a fifteen minute escalation in filth.

This is why Jesus started his ministry by coming to terms with his own temptations before he started preaching to others. He wanted to make sure he could win – before he lost. We note that his temptations were very personal to him. They were all bound up with his relationship with his Father. Temptations to disobedience which he resisted.

There is a message here for us. One of the things which

I value highly is honesty. I believe in speaking the truth openly and fearlessly. Sometimes that honesty is brutal and cutting. When I came to St Mary Magdalene's, I decided that I would always tell the congregation the truth. Things would not be said behind closed doors that could not be said publicly. Now we take it for granted that we shall speak the truth to each other. We shall be honest in our dealings with each other. This a battle which has long since been won. Perhaps you didn't even realize it was an issue?

The season of Lent is not a time for petty sacrifices. It is a time for restoring the main guidelines on which we live our lives. Not giving up sugar . . . or sweets . . . or petty things like that. But tackling our major defects. Recognizing those areas of our life where we are most likely to succumb to temptation and strengthening our defences before it is too late. To be true to ourselves. To listen to the voice of our consciences. To be stronger people. Not always to give way.

This is a spiritual battle. No one will know about it except you. The matter is a secret between you and God. The only time that other people will be aware that something has been happening will be when they see us acting differently – the way we speak – the way we behave – a sudden change in character. They will wonder how that change has occurred. The victory will be ours.

The more frequently we do a spring-clean, the cleaner a house will be. The same is true of the mind. The quicker we come to grips with our own personal temptations, the less of a mess we shall have to clear up. The easier a victory will be. Every year, the Church – following the example of Jesus – sets six weeks aside for us to clean up our act. To become better people. To renew our faith. To return to the Church. To receive the God-given sacraments. To become the Christian people we claim to be.

Surely there is a battle to be fought inside each one of us? A battle worth winning? A battle we dare not lose? To save our souls; to cleanse our minds? Or have we left it too late? Must we turn our backs on God and live another futile year? Remember what Jesus said: "There is joy in heaven over one sinner that repents." There could even be joy in our hearts. It is certainly worth trying!

(21st February 1999)

Butterflies And Things

If we had not seen such a thing, I doubt whether any of us would believe it possible! Today, a small green object with an hundred legs – and perhaps even a furry back – crawling slowly and patiently inch by inch, from blade to blade. So vulnerable; so easy to step on. Then tomorrow, a beautiful, elusive multi-coloured object with a delicate body and broad wings, flying high over the hedgerows and far away. A butterfly! A symbol of the Resurrection.

Doubtless in some parts of the world, they have never seen a butterfly. If you told them about it, they would think you were pulling their legs. How on earth can a land-based object become a high-flying thing of beauty? Surely it is not possible?

At first sight, it does seem rather ridiculous. The poor caterpillar appears to die. It is hidden away in its chrysalis. For a while nothing happens. But suddenly the chrysalis bursts open – and new life appears. So it is true. The caterpillar does become a butterfly.

Well, that may seem very much to be stating the obvious. We've all seen butterflies. We know what happens. But faced with an equally true fact – the Resurrection – we react in quite a different way. We look at it. We read about it; but disbelief clouds our minds. We say: "It can't be true." And yet it is.

The death of a human being is very like the "dying" of a caterpillar; and this should not surprise us because our Heavenly Father who made the caterpillar also made us. We also live our lives here slowly – and sometimes painfully. We are small and vulnerable. Even if we happen to be globetrotters or astronauts, we only cover in our lifetime a very small fraction of this great cosmos. And when our earthly life finishes, we too seem to enter a stage of "chrysalis" – an end to the being we have known – and perhaps loved. But we shall come to see that that was only a small part of our lives. A mere prelude . . .

In the death and resurrection of Jesus, our Heavenly Father has shown us clearly the transformation from the human caterpillar to the human butterfly. It is indeed the same Jesus – "yesterday, today and for ever." And yet it is a different Jesus.

The same markings (the wounds on the cross), the same person, the same relationship with his friends – and yet, very different. The difference lies in the "glory" of his new being. It is a body which is able to pass through walls and yet eat broiled fish. It is a body which can walk the seven miles of the road to Emmaus and yet vanish. It is a body which seems to be lit up with radiance and brightness – and yet so familiar that Mary Magdalene can reach out and touch it. Thomas could also have touched it if he had wanted to. But confronted with the reality of the Risen Christ, such proof seemed unnecessary.

In Jesus, human beings have been privileged to see what happens to a man or woman after death. Not an end or a nothingness. But, instead, a glorious creature far and away beyond our imagining. It was not for nothing that St Paul said: "Dying, and behold we live . . . "

Down here, crawling from stalk to stalk, we have hardly begun to realize what living really is. And yet, above us, before us, there lies the glorious hope of becoming new creatures – the same, but very different. No longer a prisoner of time, gravity, money, property, poor health or vile bodies . . . but free, beautiful, able to roam far and wide through this beautiful cosmos – with all eternity to do it in.

Given the example of the butterfly – given the experience of Jesus – the prospect of death (even death on a cross) should not alarm us . . . should not make us too fearful.

We – the Church – are the people who believe in butterflies. We know that the caterpillar is destined for greater things. The chrysalis of death is a mere stage in a glorious journey. This is earth. That is heaven. What a contrast! What a joy!

What a gift of God to his creatures! To the caterpillar and to all of us, St Paul says: "Awake thou that sleepest and rise from the dead, and Christ shall give thee *wings*!"

This is the great Christian message. The really good news for all caterpillars. One day, we shall all be butterflies!

(April 1991)

The Resurrection Of The Body

When Jesus was laid in the tomb on Friday night, he was dead. Of that, there is no shadow of doubt. No Roman centurion would have performed a crucifixion without making sure that superior orders were carried out in full. Legs were broken to ensure a speedy conclusion to the day's work. Before Jesus's body was removed from the cross, permission had to be obtained from Pontius Pilate himself. And a Temple guard was placed on duty outside the tomb to make quite sure nothing happened.

When Peter and John entered the tomb on Easter morning, they saw the linen clothes lying – without a body in them. The napkin which had last been seen wrapped around Jesus's head was "rolled up in a place by itself." The body had obviously gone. The stone had been rolled away. But how could anyone have taken the body without disrupting the grave-clothes? And where was the mixture of myrrh and spices – weighing about one hundred pounds – with which the body had been adorned? This is the big mystery of Easter Day.

Peter saw the linen clothes in their strange position – but did not draw any conclusion. John, we are told, "saw and believed." The two men saw the same things; but only one of them suspected resurrection. Was there any other explanation?

Surely, if you spirit a body away, you leave the coverings in a heap on the floor? Or you take them with you? When the Jews prepared a body for burial, they wrapped it up good and proper. When Lazarus emerged from the tomb, he could hardly move. He was still wrapped up in all his bandages. Jesus would have had nothing less.

So, if you have the grave-clothes all carefully wrapped around the corpse's body, and the napkin tied round his head, you cannot really get the body out without visibly disrupting all the work of preparation. There would be a mess. Spices scattered all over the floor. But what we are told is that the wrappings were still intact – but there was no body. Without seeing the Risen Christ, John believed that a resurrection had taken place.

Mary Magdalene did not believe in resurrection. She believed that somebody – most probably the gardener – had violated the special sanctity of the tomb and moved the body elsewhere. But how could that have happened with the Temple guard on duty outside the tomb? The Jewish leaders were so anxious to see Jesus dead that they spent the whole of Friday afternoon on Golgotha just to make sure. They put a guard on the tomb to prevent anything happening. The body of the dead Jesus was going to stay where it was. No mucking about!

The untouched, unwrapped grave-clothes are therefore a sign. Of themselves, they are nothing. But the clear implication of the text is that Jesus's body was, in some miraculous way, atomized where it lay. It did not rise through the grave-clothes. It did not sink through the solid rock. So what other explanation could there be?

One hundred years ago, we had no knowledge of nuclear science – but now whole cities can vanish in seconds in a nuclear explosion. Has God some secret power we do not yet comprehend which can transform our bodies from dust to glory?

One hundred years ago, we might have said "No", but now we have begun to realize how little we know about creation – and about God. Perhaps we need to be reminded of those words of Jesus: "With God, all things are possible." Even the resurrection of the dead.

(April 2001)

Daffodils Anonymous

Every year, the city of Dundee explodes in a burst of colour. Millions of daffodils proclaim the coming of Spring. Their bright yellow trumpets brave the cold winds and late frost, bringing delight and joy into the hearts of many thousands of people. We look forward to this time of year. We look forward to seeing the daffodils re-appear. Even though for most of the year, their presence is invisible to the average eye.

This morning, the Church celebrates the glory of Easter Day. The Resurrection of our Lord Jesus Christ from the dead. Like the daffodils, it is something we celebrate every year, but which always seems fresh and bright. Eight hundred million Christians celebrate this special day. And if all of us had golden trumpets – like the daffodils – what a splendid noise we should make! What a burst of praise and joy!

Like the daffodils, we have a message to proclaim. Good news for all mankind! The Church was founded to proclaim the Good News about the Resurrection. That is what we are here for. Not to bury our heads in devout piety! But to get out and proclaim: "Christ is Risen!"

Of course, many people will think we are dotty and

insane. The first Christians caused absolute amazement. How could these stupid folk be proclaiming the resurrection of a man whom everyone had seen hanging up for dead? Crucifixion was the most foolproof way of killing anyone. No one came down from the cross till they were very, very dead. The Romans knew their job backwards. When it came to killing people, they never made mistakes.

So these early Christians were regarded as very peculiar. Perhaps it was just their reaction to grief? Their way of coping with their loss? They would come round – sooner or later. So people endured their enthusiasm and hoped that before too long, they would calm down. But of course they didn't.

If you had seen green Martians landing on Riverside Drive, then you would tell people: "I saw them with my own eyes!" This was the witness of the Early Church. "I saw him with my own eyes!" Mary Magdalene came to the disciples and said: "I have seen the Lord!" But at that moment, they didn't believe her. She was a hysterical woman, just fantasizing.

If anything, resurrection made things worse. It was bad enough to see their friend crucified. Worse still to have unbalanced people playing tricks! That was the feeling of the two disciples who walked that day on the road to Emmaus. It was bad enough losing the man they had hoped would be their Messiah. But to hear rumours of angels . . . It was embarrassing and humiliating. Why couldn't they be left in peace to endure their grief?

Had the resurrection of Jesus been mere fantasy, it wouldn't have lasted more than a few days or a few weeks.

Faith is not built on froth – or dream topping. Faith is built on experience. On what people – millions of people – have seen, heard or felt. Belief comes because of that inner vision – that inner perception of the truth. A truth that dawns from the darkness – and comes alive.

The New Testament records that men and women saw Jesus alive. St Paul reports that he was seen by at least five hundred people at one time – most of whom were still alive at the time he wrote. They encountered the Risen Christ and their lives were changed. Although, after Good Friday, most of the disciples must have been thinking about returning to Lake Galilee . . . to their families . . . to their fishing . . . By the end of Easter Day, they were men with a mission. A mission to proclaim that the Man who died, lives! A message of supreme importance – not just to them – but to all mankind.

Many people have speculated about life after death. Many people have hoped it might be true. But only in the Resurrection of Jesus has that hope or dream become a reality. The Resurrection makes people think. If Jesus is alive – then perhaps I too will live on the other side of death? Perhaps life is eternal? Not, as we so often think – short, brutish and nasty! Perhaps I shall see my friends and loved ones again? Perhaps I shall even meet God himself?

Resurrection brings home to us that – like the Holy Trinity – our lives are divided into three parts, Before birth . . . the here and now . . . and what comes after. Well, we all know about being born. We know every teeny-weeny detail of how it happens. And we're here! Proof that there is indeed life after birth!

But now we're stuck in a rather uncomfortable

position, waiting for the next stage in our development. Not quite so sure about where we will be going; fearful that all our lives, all our feelings, all our love and friendship is going to end in dust. A terrifying prospect of nothingness. Just a little dust in a box.

But Jesus' resurrection has given us a pointer . . . a compass bearing . . . a helping hand . . . through our earthly pilgrimage. Death is not the end. Death – like birth – is an event in life. Death is another moment of liberation. When we throw off the shackles and limitations of our physical bodies – just as once upon a time, we threw away our umbilical cord and our embryonic sac. We didn't need them any more! One day, we shall be free of these weak, sickening bodies which, as we get older, cause us so much pain and distress. Then we shall be free.

The new life will burst from the old shell. Just as the golden daffodil bursts from the dull brown bulb, lying buried in the soil. It is difficult to believe that something so beautiful and so glorious can emerge from something that looks like a second-class onion. But it does.

It is all part of the magic and miracle of creation. God created the lot so it is not surprising that we see death and resurrection happening time and again – all around us – in every field, in every street. If God so loved plants . . . and trees . . . and flowers – bringing them back to new life year after year – is it not equally likely that he will give eternal life to all his people, who are the crown of his Creation? This is our hope. This is our joy – this Easter morning. So let a million trumpets blow! Let them proclaim: "The Lord is Risen! He is risen indeed."

(20th April 2003)

All This And Heaven, Too

If you were booked for a holiday in, say, Baalbek or Alice Springs, you would, I imagine, have some idea of what the place would be like. You would surely have looked at a brochure – or seen a picture of the hotel. You would also know the time of your flight. And presumably, you would be able to give your friends some rational explanation as to why you were going to such an outlandish place!

And yet, we are all going to a place we do not know. 90% of us are not sure if we really want to go. Nobody is able to tell us whether our destination will be terribly hot – or frightfully cold! The time and manner of our departure is unknown. And as for packing suitable clothes, it seems to be a case of "come as you are"!

The place I am speaking about is heaven. The supposed object of our Christian pilgrimage; but somewhere about which Christian theologians are notoriously vague. I actually looked up forty-five books to help me with this address. I found one excellent book on hell (written by an Episcopalian) – but nothing on heaven.

The Jews believed very much in heaven. It was the place where God lived. That place was above – above the skies. Looking up at the sky at night, the Jews thought of the stars as pinholes into heaven. It suggested to the Jews that heaven was a very bright place and the chief colour was gold. From heaven, God sent down thunderbolts . . . sunshine . . . snow. And if one wished to talk to God intimately about some important matter, one naturally went up a mountain – because up there, one was closest to God.

But the Jews did not believe that human beings went up to heaven. They wouldn't dream of such a thing. When they died, they went down to Sheol – the Pit – where they waited – perhaps for a few thousand years – for the day of their resurrection.

Their chief hope was to rise again to this world. Only the specially favoured went up to heaven. Elijah – or someone like that. But not ordinary people like us. So, because no one expected to go there, no one worried very much about what it was like.

The person who really talked about heaven in a big way was Jesus. All his parables were about "the Kingdom of Heaven." He told his hearers to lay up for themselves "treasures in heaven." He spoke of people getting their reward in heaven. In his Father's house were many rooms. He was going to prepare a place for them so that where he was, they also might be. It was believed that Jesus came down from heaven. He also ascended into heaven. So Christians rapidly came to believe that when they died, they would not be going down to the Pit, but rising up with Jesus into heaven.

St Paul added to this notion by speaking about meeting our Lord in the air. Providing us with that first picture of clouds and pearly gates which have so long blighted our picture of heaven. The Book of Revelation has also proved confusing – giving us what looks like a Hollywood set with weird creatures round a huge throne, surrounded by a crystal sea. From there, the four horsemen of the Apocalypse are sent out on their dreaded mission of bringing condemnation upon the world. There is also the heavenly Jerusalem with golden pavements and walls studded with precious stones – a fit place for the 144,000 due to be saved. What was going to happen to the rest of them, it was better not to think! They had chosen to go Lunn Poly!

None of this is really helpful. We can accept that heaven is the place where God is. We can believe it is the home of the faithful and the redeemed. We can assume that it is a place of happiness, life and joy. But we can no longer think of it as a geographical location. Nor can we think of it as "up there."

And yet, heaven is close. The writer of the book of Hebrews says that we are surrounded by a great cloud of witnesses which no man can number. These are the people who have gone before us in the faith. They are not looking down at us. They surround us. Which would seem to suggest that heaven is also around us – if we had the eyes to see and the ears to hear.

When a child is in its mother's womb, it knows of no other world than its own. Various strange sounds may reach it from outside; but they probably do not make much sense. It does not know about its father or any of its relations. It has no knowledge about what is happening next. And yet, the real world (if one may call it that) is only inches away through its mother's skin. Everybody knows about the baby – but it knows nothing about them. In the same way, we live in this womb of the world carefully shielded from reality. Knowing nothing about God.

Jacob was the first one to suspect that heaven might be found on earth. He had his vision of the staircase with angels ascending and descending. He anointed the ground where he had slept because he realized it was the gateway to heaven.

Jesus too spent his teaching ministry trying to make people realize that heaven was not something to be anticipated in the longer term – something to enjoy when you died. But something which could begin here and now. That was supposed to be the function of the Church. For people to discover a little bit of heaven in us! But do they?

"Today," Jesus said to the crook on the cross, "Today you will be with me in Paradise." Heaven is not just a future treat; but a pleasure to be enjoyed now. We do not have to wait till we are old and grey to meet God. Jesus said: Where two or three are gathered together in my name, I am in the midst of them." Heaven is closer than you think!

And there is one essential point to be made here. The closer we are to heaven in this life, the smaller step will death be. It will not be a desperate leap into the unknown, but a small step forward in a life and a relationship which has already begun.

So where do we go? Not far. A baby only moves a short way from its mother's womb to its cradle – but life then is totally different. Later, we move from the body to the spirit; but we do not move ten million miles. We are still utterly close to the ones we love – but our relation to them is of necessity different. For a little while. Until we too make our glorious way from earth to heaven.

I think half the reason why we dislike the thought of heaven is because we imagine it to be a place of boredom. Doing nothing. Sitting around. Surrounded by lots of sanctimonious, pious people. Hideous!

If, instead, we saw it as a place of dynamic activity – of doing all that we do in this life, but on a grander scale? For artists, an even brighter paint-box. For musicians, an even greater range of sounds. For lovers, even deeper joy. For carers, even more people to care for. A very dynamic heaven would be something to look forward to. A place of fulfilment. Not limbo.

If we could realize what a beautiful, splendid, exciting place heaven is, we would probably all commit suicide tomorrow. Why wait? When we could enjoy it today! It is perhaps as well that heaven's joys are veiled; because we need time to prepare for our heavenly destiny. If we could see where we were going, there would be no surprise.

So, like any holiday, we need to get ready. To prepare ourselves to make the most of it. We should rejoice at the prospect. We should convey that excitement to others.

If Christians approach death with gloom, fear, despair – that suggests that they expect very little – perhaps nothing – on the other side. Like Peter Pan, we should approach dying with the feeling that it will be "an awfully great adventure." It has been said that "hell is a state chosen by men; but heaven is a gift from God." Let us be ready to accept and enjoy that gift!

(25th May 1997)

93

Still Looking For America?

One of the most disputed facts in history is whether Christopher Columbus discovered America. Some say he did; others claim the Vikings – or even St Brendan – got there first. But whether he made it or not, the fact remains that the part of America he discovered was infinitesimally small – no more than a few square miles. Just a mere corner. There was an awful lot of America that Christopher Columbus didn't discover.

Even today, when a modern traveller can see so much more, a package holiday or even a Greyhound bus gives us no more than a series of snapshots of New York, Washington, Dallas, the Rockies, San Francisco. What we see is merely the fleeting impressions of people passing through. Four hundred years on, it would still be a brave man who could really claim to know America.

This is my starting point when I try to explain the mystery of the Trinity. We are talking about God – but it is a God that even the cleverest theologian scarcely begins to know. When you think of the vastness of the mind that created the Universe – everything from the big bang to a primrose, or an amoeba to a pit bull terrier, it is inevitably far beyond the ken of mortal men.

To say God is Father, Son and Holy Spirit – is fine as far as it goes. But that is only as far as our experience takes us. Only as far as God has been revealed. To say that God is only the Holy Trinity is for some people a very blinkered statement.

I am sure there is much, much more to God. But he remains immortal, invisible and largely unknown. He prefers it that way. He likes to keep us guessing. He has a great sense of humour.

If God were not so important, it might be better to ignore him. To say – as some people say about America – that it would have been a lot better if Christopher Columbus had left it the way it was. Undiscovered! But whilst America is a 'thing', God is a person. And human experience has shown that, in a variety of different ways, God is seeking to establish a personal relationship with each member of the human race – not by pushing himself forward – not by treating us like puppets; but by so exercising our imagination and faith, that we begin to want to discover him. However impossible the task, we set foot on one corner of the divine continent.

Different parts attract different people. Those who like trees, hills, skies, rivers, animals and nature latch on to God as Creator. As Joseph Addison's hymn says:

"The unwearied sun from day to day does his Creator's power display, and publishes to every land, the works of an almighty hand."

That part of God's creative power is there for everyone to see. It can be enjoyed, explored, developed and understood. Through it, the nature of God can be perceived. But it is only a front window. It is the easiest way in to the mystery.

Those who are inspired to create themselves, discover a different aspect of God. The Spirit who gives gifts to men and women. Gifts that range from music and writing, to inventions and theories, wisdom in its most brilliant forms. The talent to make things work. The power to speak, to think, to be able to listen, to manage, to teach, to administer. So many millions of gifts given to us all. Where do they come from? What are they all for? Why was that gift given to her? Why has my gift been given to me? Exploring the gifts of the Spirit leads us directly to the Giver; raising the question of why he should wish to dispense these gifts to us. For what purpose? Once again, we are led deeper and further into that continent of brightness and light.

Understanding Jesus is perhaps the hardest way up the mountain. At first sight, it seems easy. After all, we know what a baby is like; we can put ourselves in the disciples' place. We can hear the words of Jesus; we can look over their shoulders and watch the healings and the miracles (even if we don't quite understand how they were done). It is just about possible to see Jesus. And yet, who is this Jesus? Is he God; or is he Man? In what way do the two come together? It was precisely this question which troubled the Early Church and caused them years of disagreement and division as they tried to put together the Creeds – those statements which enshrine our beliefs. How could God become less than God?

What sort of God is it who wants to suffer and die? To be on the receiving end of creation – rather than the giving end? How can we begin to understand a God who wants to lift sinful men up to Paradise – to be with him for ever – to share his presence for eternity? Why choose us?

We know from our experience that each of us is built up from many different facets. We can be a computer engineer, a keen bowler, a husband, a father and perhaps at the same time be a non-stipendiary priest. In each facet, we show ourselves to others in different ways. And yet, we retain an inner unity. Which is the real man or woman? Is it one part? Or is it all of us?

Very often, when I am preparing for a funeral, I discover so much more about the person who has died, than I ever knew in his or her lifetime. Lots of little pictures that do not always add up. There is so much more to every human being than we realize. Each one of us is a Trinity of persons dwelling under the same roof.

Presumably, that is what the book of Genesis means when it says that God created us in his own image. It does not mean that God looks like us – although, in Jesus, we see God in human terms – in a form that we can understand and picture. It means that, in each of us, God has created a mystery, a continent waiting to be discovered. A territory where God is present – but where he is not immediately seen.

It follows that the search for God is both external and internal. In the depths of space – and in the innermost recesses of our minds. To find him – each in our own individual way – is perhaps the greatest discovery of all. Fortunately, as we start looking for God, he is looking for us. And when we do meet, it will be his joy just as much as ours.

(October 1995)

97

The First Apostle

Here in St Mary Magdalene's, when we think of the Resurrection, the first picture that comes to mind is that dramatic meeting between Jesus and Mary Magdalene in the Easter garden on the first Easter Day. The scene is beautifully displayed for us in the stained glass window in our Resurrection chapel and also in our picture at the west end of the Church. We think of her very much as our own saint.

And because Jesus chose to reveal himself to her – before anyone else – we can never doubt her importance in the Gospel story.

But when you mention her name to outsiders – to people who do not know her so well – you get a very confused response. St Mary Magdalene? She was the woman taken in adultery. She was the one who washed Jesus' feet with her hair. She was a prostitute, wasn't she? A scarlet woman? There have been a number of highly imaginative books written about her. And the infamous "Holy Blood and Holy Grail" suggested that in later life, she married Jesus and their children became the Kings and Queens of France!

Needless to say, this is all rubbish. Historically, the only evidence for Mary Magdalene is in the Bible. She appears only at the Cross and at the Tomb. She is mentioned as one of the followers of Jesus. The only slur on her character is to be found in a throw-away line in chapter 16 of St Mark's Gospel, where it is said: "Jesus appeared first to Mary Magdalene, out of whom he had cast seven devils."

Scholars agree that this section is a later addition to St Mark's Gospel. It contains many other fanciful items about disciples drinking poison and handling snakes – none of which have the ring of truth.

However, we say: "If she had seven devils, she must have been pretty bad!" But when we read the rest of the New Testament, we see that what today we call epilepsy or depression, was in those days regarded as demon possession.

If the writer is to be believed, Mary Magdalene may have been a sick woman – but we have no suggestion that she was actually bad. The trouble is that preachers and commentators have put together a composite picture of all the women Jesus met and come up with a fairly lurid picture. Then they say: "That was Mary Magdalene!" It wasn't.

Just recently, Susan Haskins, a University scholar, has produced a 518 page book exploring all the myths which have grown up surrounding this poor woman. Some of these myths have been propagated by the Church to suit its own ends. It is the absence of any real information about who Mary was that has caused all the trouble. Nature abhors a vacuum. So the first story to emerge was that she travelled to Ephesus to be with St John the Evangelist and the Virgin Mary. Here, according to one story, she became a teacher of holy women. In another, she was martyred for her faith. Tourists are still shown her house in Ephesus. Another legend says that she travelled to Marseilles with Lazarus and that she died there. Her body was apparently entombed at St Maximin-la-Sainte-Baume in Provence.

None of this would have mattered; but in the early Middle Ages, an immense cult grew up about her. It was said that her headless body had been found in Constantinople and brought back to France by the Crusaders. Her head had been buried in an altar in Rome. Her constituent parts were then brought together at a place called Vezelay, again in the south of France, where a shrine was set up and thousands of pilgrims came to see her relics. This was good for trade. Medieval people seem to have been exceptionally gullible. And Vezelay flourished for three hundred years until the church was sacked by the French Protestants and all her relics were burnt. The church was further damaged during the French revolution. So it seems unlikely that anything remains – of her remains.

But that was really nothing compared to the other things which were done to the Magdalene. The Catholic Church has always been insistent that Peter was the first disciple to see Jesus on Easter morning – despite the best evidence of Scripture. To have admitted that Mary Magdalene was the first apostle – the first to bear the Gospel message to the disciples – would perhaps have undermined that claim. So the Church was happy to see Mary Magdalene's reputation sink as that of the Blessed Virgin Mother rose. Both had stood beside the Cross.

Mary, of course, was the Mother of our Lord – so she was holy, pure and ever-virgin . . . Mary Magdalene therefore became symbolic of the more earthy kind of woman, a sinner, a temptress, sexual, beautiful but corrupt. In need of forgiveness, which she received.

This of course led to a flood of pictures – both on canvas and on stained glass, where Mary Magdalene was portrayed as a voluptuous, sensuous, fallen woman, always weeping and asking Jesus for forgiveness. The fact that Mary was crying outside the tomb was not regarded as grief – the most obvious explanation – but as a sign that she was a wretched sinner. She was transposed into the woman who washed Jesus's feet with her tears and dried them with her hair. So she was given lovely auburn hair. Painters outdid themselves to portray this loose woman. No fewer than four of Charles II's mistresses were painted as Mary Magdalene!

At the Reformation, there was a serious reaction against all this. We have a little clue to this in our Prayer Book. St Mary Magdalene, who in the Middle Ages had been regarded as a major saint, was moved to the back benches. She has a collect, epistle and Gospel for her special day – July 22nd – but it is not printed out.

She has become "a lesser saint." But this reaction was quite understandable. In the medieval Mystery plays, Mary Magdalene had been portrayed as a very colourful and immoral character. Because of her naughtiness, she had taken something away from Jesus as the central character. This could not be tolerated.

It has to be said that Mary Magdalene would not have been half as interesting if she had been a plump, middle-aged woman, grey-haired, a do-gooder – as perhaps she was.

But once you give a dog a bad name, it keeps it. People had got a picture in their minds. Mary Magdalene became the patron saint of prostitutes about seven hundred years ago. Convents and reformatories built to care for such as repented were called Magdalene's. There are places all over France called "La Madeleine."

As Nietzsche says: "every culture needs a myth." And Mary Magdalene supplied this much-needed picture of the sinner falling at the Saviour's feet. Zeferelli's film: "Jesus of Nazareth", Scorese's "Last Temptation of Christ" and even Lloyd Webber's: "Jesus Christ Superstar" keep this image alive. So as the Virgin Mary has risen ever higher in the pantheon of the Catholic Church, becoming almost untouchably divine, the passive intercessor for sinners, the Queen of Heaven . . . so Mary Magdalene has become the repository for every vice and sin imaginable. It is pure hogwash. Sentimental hogwash. But it sells.

When Bishop Forbes dedicated this Church in honour of St Mary Magdalene, he was probably thinking of the famous St Mary Magdalene's Church he had known and worshipped in at Oxford. A bastion of High Church practices. But he also probably shared the Victorian penchant for fallen women. You may remember that William Gladstone, the Liberal Prime Minister, did a great deal to try and rescue fallen women in the most respectable fashion. And Bishop Forbes – a bachelor – was a great friend of Mr Gladstone. And it was thanks to him that he was appointed Bishop of Brechin at the age of thirty.

At that time, only twenty-eight churches in England were dedicated to Mary Magdalene – but none in Scotland. It was a rather daring thing to do. Perhaps, looking at the slum population in Dundee and thinking of the high number of illegitimate children he had to baptize, Bishop Forbes was taken with the idea of the repentant sinner. It was an icon for his time.

Interestingly enough, in recent years, Mary Magdalene has moved back from sinner to saint. Her role as the first witness of the Resurrection has been taken on board by feminists as a good example for women's ministry in the Church. Her primacy as an apostle has been recognized and she has now become the prototype liberated woman!

We have come back to the view that she must have been more than a reject or a sinner. She must have loved Jesus – but for what he was, not just because he was a man and she was a woman. He had seen her faith – her great faith – and welcomed it. Her courage. Her loyalty. Therefore he had chosen her especially to be the first apostle. It is now seen the be one of the great sins of Church history that she has been misrepresented so falsely – probably with a view to devaluing a woman's role in the life and ministry of the Church.

Whether this new image is true or false, it suits the needs of our time. Once again, Mary Magdalene can be used to project our latest whims and fancies. Surely the time has come to lift her out of the realms of fantasy and restore to her rightful place – as simply a friend of Jesus. Just a friend. Someone who cared enough for him to stand beside his Cross on Good Friday afternoon, when all the male disciples – except St John – had run away.

Someone who came to the Tomb to grieve, but who in her sorrow, was privileged to meet the Risen Christ.

That should be enough! But I can guess – and I would even bet – that come the next fashion or trend in the Church, Mary of Magdala will be taken on board to make some ecclesiastical point.

We often criticize the gutter press for making something out of nothing, But the Church has constantly done the same. Quite inappropriate people have been elected to the sainthood for political, religious or social reasons. Joan of Arc is a case in point. There is every reason to believe that she did not die at the stake.

Her memorial stone still graced a church in eastern France until the early twentieth century stating that she had married and died in 1456. But, we may note that she was accorded sainthood to make the Church more attractive to the French people at a time of defeat and despair. Her canonization took place in 1920 – just after the First World War.

Mary Magdalene has only a small part in the Gospel story. But a vital part. It is one of the great events which took place on the first Easter Day. Her witness to the Resurrection of Jesus should be honoured and respected. More than that – further than that – we should not go. In fact, it would do no harm if we could try to set the record straight. Once and for all.

(13th April 1997)

As Pants The Hart

Very soon, it will be the Glorious Twelfth – an event still celebrated in Scotland – when a large number of birds will be shot and other animals hunted down for pleasure. It happens every year. It is part of our rich national heritage. In time past – perhaps even today – the Royal Family take a prominent part in this sport.

In Bosnia, snipers happily mow down men, women and children – and they are condemned. But we in this country happily condone the death of thousands of wild animals and birds because blood sports are part of our tradition. We say that animals are different to human beings. They are – quite literally – fair game!

It is, I think, a moral question and one on which Christians should take a stand. As a nation, we are famous for our love of animals. Dogs and cats are lovingly protected. This country was the first to have an organization specifically founded for the prevention of cruelty to animals. The founder of our Church, Bishop Forbes, was the man who brought the RSPCA to Dundee. And our strong feelings reach out to other nations. To donkeys maltreated in Spain; to dancing bears in Turkey; to the inhuman treatment of horses.

Some of you will remember that, a few years ago, there was immense concern about three whales stuck in the Arctic ice. The whole world was concerned about their survival. In recent years, Britain has played a major part in trying to end commercial whaling. Long ago, we put an end to bear-baiting and cock-fighting. But we still tolerate blood sports. The public outcry is limited to the Animal Liberation Front and a few other cranks.

Now if some young thug from Kirkton – or Broughty Ferry – went around shooting stray cats or dogs; if he boasted that he had brought down 2000 sparrows and pigeons in a single weekend, he would undoubtedly be pilloried in the press. He would be called a sadist and there would hopefully be steps taken to prosecute him for wilful cruelty.

But because it is part of our social custom to hunt and shoot . . . because people dress up for the occasion . . . because titled people, businessmen and the Royal Family are involved, there are no public accusations of cruelty or sadism for what they do. No prosecutions. No condemnation by the Church. But morality is not divisible. If it is wrong to kill, it is wrong full stop. The sixth commandment says: "You shall not kill." It doesn't specify whether it means animals or humans. It covers both.

Not so long ago, it was considered quite fashionable to hunt big game and elephants. The rarer the animal killed, the greater the feather in the huntsman's cap. In 1961, there was a terrible outcry when Prince Philip, as part of a royal entertainment, shot a rare white rhinoceros in India. As President of the World Wildlife Fund, it was felt to have been an act of crass hypocrisy.

But the hypocrisy and the double standards live on. Because wild animals are becoming scarce, we now realize their value. We go to enormous lengths to preserve species and conserve them. There is justifiable anger at the decision of Norway and Japan to resume whaling. But no one lifts a finger to prevent the stag, the fox, the pheasant and the grouse from being the victim of systematic slaughter.

Like you, I have heard all the arguments about controlling pests like foxes . . . how much worse it would be to gas them or poison them. I have heard it said that the Monarchs of the Glens can become very destructive and need to be culled. We have all heard the argument that if it wasn't for the shoots, grouse and pheasants wouldn't be bred; people would lose their jobs; estates would close; visitors wouldn't come to Scotland for the "sport." But that is not really the point!

To eat, man has to kill. We do it reluctantly as a necessity. We do it as humanely as possible. The Bible does not encourage us to be vegetarians. The Bible has many stories of people hunting or fishing for food. That is not condemned. But killing for pleasure is different.

Racing can be justified in the sense that both horse and rider take part with an equal risk of breaking their necks. But the grouse does not have an equal chance of shooting back! The salmon fisher is in no danger of getting a nasty hook down his throat. The stag does not have the benefit of telescopic sights to keep an eye on his pursuer. It is not sport – it is organized murder. And it is wrong – just as slavery was wrong. Even though everyone did it; even though all the "best people" had vested interests in slavery continuing – it had to be stopped.

The people of Africa have now discovered that people

want to come out to Africa not to go on safari and kill; but to admire the wild life in their natural habitat. To consider the lifestyle of the animals. We can do without ivory. We do not need to have rhinoceroses' feet as waste paper baskets! Film stars can manage without a tiger's head on the floor or the skin of a grizzly on the wall! Internationally, we are becoming much more civilized.

Animals will still have to be killed. Birds will have to be shot. If whales become too numerous, they may again have to be culled. But there is a great difference between killing for food, killing to control numbers and killing that is part of a social ritual for which people pay; which people enjoy and which is considered socially correct.

Living in a city, we stand apart from these things. We are told that living in the countryside is different. That we do not understand rural life. I would suggest that it is because we stand in a detached position, we are able to see the immorality more clearly.

Time and custom do not hallow wrong-doing. Just because it has always been done is no excuse. It is something which is a slur and a shame on the face of Britain. It is most certainly not the "Glorious" Twelfth! It is something which should be eradicated from our culture just as surely as we shun bull-fighting or the Roman practice of slaughtering animals in the Colosseum. We should know better.

Coming to Church is thought by some to be an escape from reality. An opportunity to forget the hardness and cruelty of the real world. But we cannot escape reality. We cannot ignore the voice of conscience. We have to speak out. The Church has always been in the forefront of campaigns to put an end to immorality and cruelty.

This is one of the nastiest leftovers of primitive society and we should not hide our eyes away from it just because the Royal Family do it and some Scottish estates depend on hunting and fishing to make money.

Before we condemn the snipers in Sarajevo and the mass murderers in Srebrenica, let us consider what is being done on our own doorstep! Morality begins at home; and until we have dealt with our own problems, we are in no position to judge others. The killing must stop.

(12th July 1992)

Surprise! Surprise!

For the past fourteeen years, I have paid regular visits to this Crematorium. And each time I come here, there is a heaviness in my heart. Because I know that for all the people I shall be meeting here, there is an ending. An ending of hopes and dreams. An ending of a long and happy relationship between husband and wife, between parents and child, between neighbours and friends. We may have shut our minds to the reality of death – but in this place, we are reminded of the truth of those words in the book of Genesis: "Dust thou art and unto dust shalt thou return."

We try to forget that we are mortal. When we are young, we think our bodies will last for ever. We cherish them, pamper them, constantly indulge them. We think how well we are doing. A good job. A nice home. A happy family. A secure pension. A healthy lifestyle. Years of pleasure and satisfaction lie ahead. But coming to this crematorium reminds us that men and women do not last for ever. Our bodies decay. Muscles fail. The pump stops. Our vital parts may be destroyed by cancer or some other foul disease. We die.

That is the bad news. Now for the good news! Man is

certainly made from dust. His body is a perishable item. But we are more than dust. To each of us, God has given a spirit – something imperishable – which cannot be destroyed. So, when the body finally claps out, the spirit returns to the person who gave it. The spirit lives on.

This experience is not entirely unknown to us. In the old days, when milk came to us in bottles rather than the new plastic containers, the milkman was a regular visitor to our front doorstep. He left the milk. We drank the contents. And next morning, he collected the empties and took them back to the dairy. It is much the same idea with God – expect, of course, it is the other way round! We use the bottle. Then we return the contents!

It seems odd. You would think the most natural thing would be to consume the contents and then give God the bottle. Eat the orange and give God the skin. But it is the other way round. It is the body which is disposable – not the spirit. The spirit returns to God.

One of the chief objects of the Christian faith has been to try and help ordinary people to understand God. That was one of the chief objects of Jesus's ministry. To teach people about the Kingdom of God. All his parables were designed to show how God worked. That he cared for one lost sheep more than for the ninety-nine. That it was easier for a camel to go through the eye of a needle than for a rich man to enter the Kingdom of heaven. That we should love our enemies. Turn the other cheek . . . When Jesus talked to people, there were constant gasps of surprise. Because he turned conventional views about God upside down.

Jesus showed us that whatever we think about God is

probably wrong! This is a fairly good maxim. Whatever we think is probably wrong. Because we tend to think of God as a rather superior version of ourselves. We think this way – so, we presume, he does as well. We say: "We couldn't possibly do that!" so we assume God couldn't do it either. The virgin conception, the healing miracles, the resurrection all raise doubts and disbelief because they are outside our own immediate experience. But, as Jesus said: "With God all things are possible."

Even raising the dead!

So this gives us a starting point for our Memorial Service this afternoon. We are dust. God knows that we are dust. But he has managed to transform that dust into some very advanced bodies. Some beautiful shapes. Some wonderful minds. You only have to look at your hand and think of all the tiny cells, blood vessels, muscles and intricate bones which go together to make up its structure to realize that an object containing such detailed design cannot "just happen" – even with all the benefits of evolution. There has to be a master mind behind creation. Things just do not happen of their own accord. Our bodies are truly miraculous.

But so are our spirits. The inner thoughts, feelings, love, skills, talents which develop and blend together to create our own unique personalities. Something that is essentially "me." There is already an inter-reaction between God and ourselves in the voice of conscience – that inner-knowing what we should or should not do. We can override it. We can ignore it. But there is a bit of global-positioning going on day-by-day as God helps us on our way and gives us flashes of insight or gently nudges us in the right direction. But we remain our own bosses. God has given all of us free will and it is up to us to do good or evil. Most of us do good.

We need to remember that God has created us to be his friends. Not just in this world. But in the world to come. As the clergy never cease to remind us, this life is only a preparation for the life that is to come. We spend nine months preparing to be born. And we spend 70, 80 – perhaps even 90 years – preparing to die.

Death is an important event in life. *In life!* The Venerable Bede once described death as "our spiritual birthday." It is the moment when, having disposed of the bottle, we begin to enjoy being the real people we are – without the distractions and disabilities our bodies have imposed upon us all these years. Now we can travel to the moon without needing a spaceship. Now we can see all our friends and loved ones who have gone before us into heaven. Now we can see God. If he looks like Jesus, do not be surprised! Jesus is the human face of God.

So our spirits need to be nurtured. Because these are the things which are going to survive. Not the bodies! If we spent as much time looking after our spirits as we do looking after our bodies, we might be better prepared.

So often we hand back to God a blank canvas. In our earthly lives, we may have had a large bank balance, a beautiful house, an important job – but suddenly these things don't count any more. We discover that what matters is how much we cared for people. Were we good Samaritans – or did we walk by on the other side? Did we forgive . . . ? Did we even love anyone but ourselves? Hopefully, by the time we get to heaven, we shall have something on our canvas! Something to show that we have not completely wasted our time down here.

Now let us put all these thoughts together. They do not suggest an ending. Rather they suggest that there is more to be enjoyed. A new life. Certainly, a different life – with different values and different expectations. God has something better in store. What was it that Jesus said to his disciples? "Not even a sparrow falls to the ground without your heavenly Father noticing . . . " And then a little smile. "Fear not, you are of more value than many sparrows!" God values us more highly than perhaps we deserve. So he is not going to leave us in the dust of death.

These are comforting words on an afternoon such as this. This Crematorium is a bit like the wedding in Cana of Galilee. It is a place with no wine. No hope; no joy; no life. This is where so many parties have come to an end. When the people we love are gone; where everything precious is reduced to dust. But it is just at this moment that God springs his greatest surprise. In a place of absolute despair, God brings out his new wine – his greatest miracle. The gift of eternal life.

Well might the steward say in the story: "You have kept the best wine till now!" This is the way God chooses to operate. He waits till we have reached the end of the road – till we have well and truly hit the buffers – till all human hope is gone. Then he comes to our aid.

For us, a crematorium symbolizes death and tears. But in God"s eyes, it is a gateway to heaven. From this empty tomb, our resurrection life begins. Jesus said:

"I am the Resurrection and the Life. He who believes in me – even though he were dead, yet shall he live; and whoever lives and believes in me will never die."

This is the very core of our Christian belief. Let us not just believe it . . . but also live as if we believed it. Let us make Resurrection life a reality now – just as it is already a reality for our loved ones who now know that God's promises are true.

(7th November 1982)

Lake Galilee

This has been a long and miserable winter. So, this morning, I thought I would take you far away from Dundee and set you down beside Lake Galilee, the place where Jesus did so much of his teaching and healing.

The word "Galilee" comes from a Greek word meaning "a circle". In fact, the Lake is not a circle. It is thirteen miles long and eight miles wide. It is about eight times bigger than Loch Lomond. We imagine Galilee high up in the hills of Palestine; but in fact, it is actually 682 feet beneath the sea level of the Mediterranean.

The water which fills the Lake comes from the surrounding hills and mountains. And because it comes from the hills, the water is icy cold – even on a summer's day. Even today, Lake Galilee supplies 45% of the water needs of the State of Israel.

So it is not just a pretty sight. The Lake is of great strategic importance – which is why the Israelis are extremely reluctant to hand back the nearby Golan Heights to Syria. As in the days of old, whoever controls the Lake of Galilee controls the whole country.

From the Lake flows the famous River Jordan – sixty-five miles long. It flows straight down a broad, lush valley till it reaches the Dead Sea – which is indeed a large inland sea – full of salty water – fifty-three miles long and ten miles wide. The two stretches of water could not be more different. Because of the mineral salts in the Dead Sea, it is – as its name suggests – devoid of all life. But the sea of Galilee is simply teeming with fish. There are seventeen different varieties of fish to be found there; and even today, 1800 tons of fish are extracted each year from Lake Galilee.

As in biblical times, you will still see fishermen mending their nets beside the seashore, because the bed of the Lake is full of very sharp stones which tear the nets. In fact, one might say that if you were going to cross Lake Galilee, it would be much more pleasant to walk on the water than to walk on the stones.

Of all the fish in the Lake, the most unusual is perhaps the comb fish – about six inches long – which is sometimes called St Peter's fish. This species has the rather unusual habit of carrying its eggs in its mouth for protection purposes and, apparently, the fish carries in its mouth a stone or pebble to stop it swallowing its young.

This explains what I have always found one of the most difficult of all the Bible stories. In St Matthew, chapter 17, the disciples arrive at the local customs post without any money. Jesus tells Peter to cut open a fish and he will find a coin in its mouth. He should use that coin to pay their customs due. I always found that story very hard to believe. But when you know about the habits of this particular fish, it seems quite within the bounds of possibility that the mouth of the fish could contain a small coin instead of a pebble.

Galilee is like Dundee in that it experiences very strong winds. The surrounding hills create a sort of cauldron effect and the winds sweep round and round the hills till they descend violently on the Lake transforming a peaceful, idyllic setting into a raging storm. It is therefore quite understandable that Jesus could have been lying sleeping in a boat one minute – and the next, the vessel could be thrown backwards and forwards – in danger of sinking. The Lake was – and still is – a dangerous place for amateurs. Even the professional fishermen are sometimes caught napping.

We notice in the Gospels that the disciples were not always very successful in their fishing. "Master, we have toiled all night and taken nothing!" Even today, the fishermen of Lake Galilee still fish by night. This is because the water is so bright and clear that any fish can see a net coming and escape. So the fishing is done at night.

In biblical times, the Lake was surrounded by a number of so-called cities with populations of 15,000 and more. There was Cana of Galilee where Jesus turned the water into wine. Capernaum where he preached in the synagogue. And Bethsaida where he performed many miracles. There was also the city of Tiberias built by the local Jewish king, Herod Antipas, to impress the Romans. It was renowned for its hot springs. As the name suggests, it was built in honour of the Emperor and its population was mostly non-Jews.

At that time, as St John reminds us, the Lake was renamed "The Sea of Tiberias". But whereas emperors come and go, the Lake remains the same; and the city of

Tiberias is now no more than a heap of rubble. In the Old Testament, Lake Galilee is mentioned only six times. It did not play a large part in the history of Israel. Jerusalem was the place where things happened.

But, for us Christians, the events which happened in and around that Lake have shaped our minds and left a very clear picture indeed. We think of Jesus preaching to the people from a boat. We think of him going up into the hills to pray. We think of him telling the fishermen to launch out into the deep. We think of that ghostly scene when he came across the waves to his disciples in the middle of the night. We think of him speaking of living water.

We think of the fish cooking on the seashore after the Resurrection. "Come and have breakfast . . . " All these images – and many more – spring from his ministry in and around the Lake. It was very much part of his life; and through the Gospels it has become ours as well.

"O Sabbath rest by Galilee!

O calm of hills above,

Where Jesus learnt to share with thee

The silence of eternity,

Interpreted by love."

But it was not always like that. The Galileans had a reputation for violence and rebellion. When Jesus was a boy, the people in the Galilean town of Sepphoris rose up against the Romans. Their revolt was severely punished. The women and children were sold into slavery; such men as were captured were crucified and their crosses were placed on the high ground overlooking Galilee so that everyone would be reminded of the cost of rebellion.

When Jesus called upon his followers to take up their cross and follow him, he would have been thinking of those men of Sepphoris. That is perhaps why Jesus was regarded as so dangerous by Caiaphas and the Jewish authorities. Was he another Galilean rebel? Another would-be Messiah? Would he bring more violence and bloodshed to the country? One can perhaps understand the High Priest's anxiety and his insistence that "one man should die so that the nation would be saved."

It is perhaps worth noting that after the resurrection, the disciples were told that Jesus would meet them in Galilee. "It is there you will see him." This message found its fulfilment in St John, chapter 21 where Jesus and his disciples were reunited on the seashore. A moment of peace and serenity before they returned to the city of Jerusalem with all its dangers and cruel memories. For us too, Galilee reminds us that, amidst all the strife and anxiety we experience in our everyday lives, the Risen Christ can still be found, sharing with us the comfort and joy of his resurrection life:

"Drop thy still dews of quietness,

Till all our strivings cease;

Take from our souls the strain and stress,

And let our ordered lives confess

The beauty of thy peace."

(6th March 1994)

God Under The Microscope

One of the interesting things – perhaps the only interesting thing – to emerge from the recent American election was the question of stem cell research. The question was raised after the sudden death of Christopher Reeve who, after his accident, had campaigned actively for stem cell research. It was not to be expected that, in the course of a bruising election campaign, such an issue would be seriously debated. But the fact that such research is opposed by so many Christians in the USA – and by the so-called moral majority in the Republican establishment – did raise in my mind a slight scintilla of doubt as to whether George Bush was the right man to be President of such a large and important country!

It seems that whenever we are faced with fresh scientific discoveries, Christians are always the first to oppose, reject and scoff at new ideas. The prime example of this was Galileo, the Italian astronomer and mathematician, who proved beyond the shadow of a doubt that the earth revolved around the sun. He faced the Inquisition. He was summoned to Rome, threatened with torture, jailed and forced to recant. His work was condemned and put on the Index of Forbidden Books till 1757.

Then again, when Darwin published his famous book: "The Origin of Species" in 1859 and "The Descent of Man" twelve years later, the Church was virulently opposed to the whole notion of evolution. Even today – in Scotland – schools are being set up which teach "creationism', saying that the world came ready-made with no evolution whatsoever.

It is widely believed – especially by some evangelical Christians – that the laws of science undermine the laws of God. There is an enormous fear that science might disprove Christianity. Therefore it is better to shut one's ears and close one's mind. There seems to be an odd feeling amongst Christian people that God needs to be protected as if he – or she – was an endangered species! If it wasn't so sad, it might be funny.

But the ignorance and fear generated by such views does Christianity no good . . . no good whatsoever. People forget that biology, physics and chemistry are the divine tools which God used to create this world – and to create us.

I have a little book on my bookshelf – published in 1940 – almost prehistoric! It is entitled: "Why smash atoms?" It was a good question – in 1940! Scientists have smashed atoms to discover the deepest secrets of life itself. The micro-elements which are contained in the tiniest building blocks of life.

And their discoveries have not destroyed the Christian faith one iota. Rather, their discoveries have led us to marvel at the detail, the complexity, the beauty which can be found in every particle of matter.

We no longer need to ask whether it is true that Jesus

did the miracles he did. We know that every aspect of life is a miracle. Every cell . . . every electron . . . a thing of wonder. As Jesus said in our reading this morning: "With God, all things are possible." Even the virgin birth is no longer a mystery! It can be achieved today in a laboratory – if not yet in a stable!

It seems to me that Christians should welcome all forms of scientific discovery which open up our belief, which deepen our understanding, which give us an even greater sense of wonder that God has gone to such trouble to create solar systems, planets, chemical compounds, chromosomes and quarks – things of which only now we are becoming aware. These things amplify our understanding of those opening words of the Creed:

"I believe in one God, the Maker of heaven and earth, and of all things visible and invisible . . . "

It seems that many of these wonders are invisible to the naked eye – but quite clear under the microscope.

This is the God we are worshipping. Not the God of Abraham, Isaac and Jacob – a tribal deity. But the everloving Creator who brought us from the big bang to the primrose. From the simple amoeba to the infinitely complex human brain which is still more compact and more powerful than any computer. And please note, God did it without any help from Bill Gates!

Science is no threat to our faith. It illuminates it. It enriches it. I think it was Albert Einstein who said: "Your God is too small!" So often, he is. Which means our faith, too, is narrow and blinkered. Christians seem to want to confine God to the pages of the Bible; to the four walls of a Church; rather than recognize his cosmic omnipotence as Creator and Sustainer of all.

We have to remember that the God we worship at Christmas time – the Word made flesh – is involved in everything. We are only a part – an important part – but only a part of his great plan for the world. Jesus said: "I came that you might have life – and have it more abundantly." We are part of a divine adventure.

And so we return to stem cell research, to cloning, to replacing defective genes, to improved IVF, designer babies – and all the rest! Of course it is controversial. Of course it raises serious moral issues. It means that we are tampering with creation, exercising God-like authority in matters of life and death. Because it is science some people think it is wrong.

But believe me, what is happening in Iraq . . . in the Sudan . . . in Zimbabwe . . . is infinitely worse from a moral point of view. Scientists are trying to save life – to improve it. Far worse is the slaughter of innocent people, starving them, tearing down their homes, suicide bombing . . . for which politicians are responsible. That seems to be a far greater evil which we are incapable of solving. By comparison, the dangers of stem cell research seem very small – very innocent.

I ask you: "Should we not be working with God trying to improve the defects in creation – rather than ignoring them?" If we could devise a gene which would stop people fighting, would that not be a blessing? What would the born-again Christians say about that? Would they say that was interfering? Going against human nature?

Perhaps. But perhaps there is a chemical solution to sin? If we find it, should we use it to save mankind? That would be a very interesting question!

However, in the meantime, let us not be like the Christian leaders in time past, burying our heads in the sand, blind to the world of nature and science – out of fear ... out of ignorance ... out of bigotry. Our battle is not just a battle against sin, but against microbes and viruses, cancer cells, defective chromosomes, genetic disorders, human infertility. These are just as much Christian battles as the fight against poor housing, bad drains, malaria, mumps, cholera, polio, diphtheria – battles of the 19th and 20th century which have already been fought and won.

It is amazing that Americans will oppose stem cell research – and at the same time shut their eyes to the more awesome danger of pollution and global warming. A cloned baby is nothing in comparison with the melting of the polar ice cap! Yet both issues require enlightened leadership and a willingness to tackle the very frontiers of human knowledge.

Let us remember that God is infinitely greater than we can ever begin to realize. His whole life is full of change, development, bringing new worlds into being. We have been called to be his partners and friends in this great cosmic adventure. To chicken out is to turn our backs on the glory of God and the great miracle of Life itself. Surely this would be the greater sin?

(7th November 2004)

I'm Not Superstitious, But . . .

It has been said that one man's religion is another man's superstition. That is how it may appear. A savage kneeling in front of a tree which he believes contains the spirits of his ancestors. A Christian kneeling before a wooden altar on which are the sacraments of eternal life. The question is: "Which one is true?"

Belief is something good and positive. Superstition is concerned with fear and anxiety; warding off invisible evil and propitiating some hidden force which may have the power to hurt us – or even kill us. We cross our fingers – just in case. We touch wood – just in case. We avoid walking under ladders – just in case.

Now, if you genuinely believe that something nasty might happen, such provisions are logical and sensible. But if you believe such things are not true – and not real – then your reactions are quite irrational. They are a response to some sub-conscious psychological fear – perhaps a living relic of some ancient religion. The reason for doing such things long forgotten.

For instance, we are told that it is seven years bad luck to break a mirror. I once broke two mirrors in the course of a month and never suffered the slightest misfortune.

Almost perversely, I have always walked under ladders – preferably as many as possible! In fact, I am almost superstitious about defeating superstition!

Breaking a mirror was an extension of an old custom of not destroying one's reflection in a pool or lake . . . because the water was supposed to have some healing power. Therefore, to destroy one's reflection was to destroy one's soul. Can you really believe such things?

Then again, the supposed good fortune of having a black cat walk across one's path. (Or a white cat if you live in America.) Cats are supposed to be familiars of witches. A cat on a boat at sea is also a good sign. If a cat sneezes near a bride on her wedding morning, it is supposed to ensure a happy married life. If, however, the family cat should sneeze three times, it is a sure sign that the entire family is going to succumb to some collective illness. Can you really believe such things?

In Scotland, we are particularly prone to superstition. If there are two funerals, people will say that a third one will soon be on the way. Often, this is true. But, in my experience, it is not a general rule.

At a funeral in the Highlands, it is dangerous to retrace one's steps. A clergyman I knew ordered the pall-bearers back into church at Ballachulish because it was snowing. There was much grousing about going back indoors; and, sure enough, one of the pall-bearers died less than three months later. It was the clergyman's fault. He was obliged to leave the parish.

I am often told it is dangerous to leave one's Christmas decorations up after the Twelfth night. Perhaps I might also point out (for the benefit of Dundee City Council) that it is also extremely unlucky to put up one's Christmas decorations before Christmas Eve. (Putting them up in early November is really asking for it!)

At New Year, we still have the ancient custom of "first-footing". A sure sign of good luck and prosperity. But the first-foot must never be a woman nor must it be someone who is flat-footed, cross-eyed or a person with eyebrows which meet over the bridge of the nose! Preferably, it should be a tall, dark, handsome stranger bearing bread or coal. A bottle of Famous Grouse – though obviously welcome – would be no substitute!

The old Scottish custom of bringing a child to Church on its first trip outside the front door was not done out of piety. It was pure superstition. The idea was that the child was in peril from witches and evil spirits who might pinch its name. Iron, salt or garlic were hidden in its shawl to ward off the evil eye. The baptismal "piece" was also a defence against evil. It was handed to the first person one saw of the opposite sex on the way to the church. To refuse the "piece" was a bad omen.

If a baby cried when the water was poured over him, everyone was happy. That was a sign of the devil coming out of him. If a baby was silent, the devil was still there. The baby might be sick – or die. Baby boys were baptized first so that they might grow beards. Girls were baptized second to avoid such a tragedy. Can you really believe such rubbish?

And yet, many people wear crosses round their necks as lucky charms. Evangelical Christians are said to open their Bibles at random and pinpoint a verse – deciding on the strength of that gamble what the word of the Lord is.

We count our plum stones to determine our future: "This year, next year, sometime, never . . . "

The 13th day is said to be unlucky. Especially if it is a Friday. Some people refuse to live in a house numbered 13. I live in No 14 Albany Terrace and I can honestly declare that no visible tragedy has afflicted my neighbours in the past twelve years. (After I had preached this sermon, it was pointed out that my neighbours in No 13 had had the misfortune of living next to me!)

Yet this superstition is very prevalent. If you go to Ninewells Hospital, you will not find a Ward 13. Hospital administrators – otherwise such rational and sensible people – were so superstitious that they avoided it. And God help you if you take red and white flowers into a hospital ward. It is a sure sign of death for someone. And yet people die in hospital every day. You wouldn't think that a red and a white gladioli would make all that much difference!

At a dinner party of politicians, a hostess refused to start a meal with only thirteen guests. Surely they couldn't have been so concerned about Judas Iscariot being the thirteenth person at the Last Supper? Today, people are refusing to buy cars with the registration number 666 because it is the supposed number of the great beast in the book of Revelation. People are supposed to have had nasty accidents in cars with that number. Can you really believe such things?

At weddings, horseshoes are given for good luck. Why do people give horseshoes when they have no horses to go with them? Apparently, it is a moon sign – the crescent moon which should in no circumstances be looked at through glass. Iron is reportedly a lucky metal; fire a primitive spirit and the nail holes reminiscent of the wounds Jesus bore on the cross.

A green car is also reported to be unlucky. And how many women avoid wearing a green dress? The ace of spades is a sign of death. A four-leaved clover will bring you good luck. "Red sky at night is the shepherd's delight; red sky in the morning is the shepherd's warning." For God's sake, don't drop a pair of scissors! Say your Rosary three times. Make sure you have your lucky pen with you when you're doing your examination paper. Don't spill your Saxa salt. And never kill a spider. "If you wish to live and thrive, let the spider run alive!" What a load of old cobblers!

Later this week, many people will be celebrating Halloween – a daft time when people pay lip service to the supposed powers of darkness which Christianity is supposed to have swept away long ago. We seem to have invented a devil with God-like powers. Perhaps in these days of sex equality, we should have a Mrs Devil as well?

The Christian faith can so easily be turned into superstition. Even St Columba added to it by suggesting that at Christmas midnight all the animals and birds took on a human voice to praise God. We absorb these little stories. "Blessed is the bride on whom the sun shines. Blessed is the corpse on whom the rain pours." Having done a committal at a graveside during a hailstorm, I can tell you it was certainly no blessing!

I am sorry to go on . . . But even making a will is supposed to be unlucky. (And yet it is something we should all do.) Opening an umbrella in a house is highly provocative. (To whom?) We encourage children to put teeth under their pillow for the tooth fairy. (Who never comes.) We stir our Christmas puddings clockwise to ward off the evil one . . . and we put in pieces of silver for good luck.

Kindly note that in our Creed we do not say: "I believe in the Devil." Worshipping or even suggesting the existence of a cosmic devil is not part of our Christian faith. It is a part of Persian mythology; but some Bible Christians will tell you – with the utmost sincerity – that Satan is alive and walking the earth. I am sorry to disappoint them. There is no place for a devil in a world where God is good.

Thomas Aquinas, the greatest theologian of the Middle Ages, said that all superstition is contrary to religion because it offers worship and respect either to whom it ought not to be offered or in a manner in which it should not be offered.

Belief in any power but God is superstition. Fear in what may happen – is not faith. Luck and bad luck is not faith. Warding off supposed evil spirits is not faith. Reading your horoscope by Mystic Meg is not faith. (Though most of us do it "just for fun!") They are all instances of that half world of fear and uncertainty from which we mature Christians are supposed to have escaped. St John said: "Perfect love casts out fear." But superstitions put us back into bondage; to elemental shadows of things which go bump in the night. It leads us back to witchcraft, sticking pins in wax dolls, black magic, potions, charms and spells.

Belief is a thing of light, joy and laughter. Faith is

something positive and hopeful. St Paul reminded us that the most important things in life are "faith, hope and love." They are good things which last for ever. They will never hurt anyone. Superstition is dark, dread, evil, negative, fearful, damaging to people's lives. It prevents them doing the good things they could be doing. President Franklin D. Roosevelt once said: "The only thing we have to fear – is fear itself."

So, turn your back on such stupidities. Believe in a real God, a real world, a world where you can sleep peacefully at night. A God to whom you can pray. A God whom you can trust. Not in the salvation of crossing your fingers, touching a piece of wood or walking round ladders! But in a God who has already rescued us from sin and evil and has given us the promise of eternal life.

Have faith - not fear!

(27th October 1991)

Peace

I don't know about you, but if there is one word which
makes me groan, it is the word: "Peace". Every time a
clergyman rises on his hind legs and says: "Let us pray, "
I know precisely what we will be praying for. "Let us pray
. . . for the peace of the world." I don't know how many
times I have been invited to pray for the peace of the
world, but I can tell you this, the invitation is rapidly
becoming counter-productive. For I have now got to the
point that when someone says: "Let us pray for the peace
of the world . . . " I say: "Oh, no! Not again!"

And yet it is such a reasonable prayer. There is surely
no better thing we could pray for. There is nothing we
want more. Peace in our homes. Industrial peace. Peace
in the Middle East. An end to suicide bombings and global
terrorism. To be able to watch the television news without
that constant litany of death. Peace. Peace at any price.

The politicians of the world know that longing. They
know what we want. Have you ever heard a political
speech yet, that did not contain the magic word: "Peace"?

To hear them speak, one would believe that peace was
something to which they alone held the key. How often
have we heard those words which Neville Chamberlain

uttered on his return home from Munich: "I believe it is peace for our time . . . peace with honour." Some years ago, I remember, the Soviet Union launched "a peace offensive"!

I think for most of us, the best definition would be "an absence of conflict." No strikes. No wars. No vandalism. No crises. No rows. No noise. If everything was peaceful, things would move much more smoothly. We should enjoy life more.

No one would criticize. No one would disturb us. We should be free – to be ourselves. Put like that, peace sounds rather like a vacuum. A vague, empty but rather happy thing – which we can fill with whatever we want. Abstract – with animal, vegetable and mineral connections! Is this what we are praying for? Is this what we want to see in the world?

Nature, we are told, abhors a vacuum. And so does man. If you create a demilitarized zone, someone is bound to want to put a gun or two into it. If you create a blank stretch of wall (as Dundee City Council knows only too well) someone is bound to cover it with paint. Find a stretch of beautiful countryside and someone will want to build a housing estate in it or create a caravan park. Enjoying a quiet Sunday morning in bed? You can be sure someone has got up early to trim their garden hedge! So if you want peace that is a vacuum – an emptiness – you are bound for disappointment. You will never get peace. You will always fail.

This is why Jesus said to his disciples: "The peace I am going to give you is not the sort of peace the world gives you . . . " I am not going to offer you some vague, nebulous thing. An illusion . . . I am going to give you real peace. Not a vacuum; but a presence. I am going to give you the Holy Spirit. The Comforter. Someone who will fill you with new life – with the Resurrection life that I have. So that you may have it too. "My peace I give unto you . . . "

The peace that Jesus was offering was not a quick deal worked out over a business lunch or at a summit between the great powers; but that deeper peace and contentment when the Holy Trinity comes to live with us. When God makes our heart – his home. Jesus said: "if a man loves me, he will keep my word. And my Father will love him and we will come to him and make our home with him."

If you have a holy man coming to your house, that man brings peace. Not his peace – but God's peace. I was very conscious of this when Archbishop Anthony Bloom, the Metropolitan of the Russian Orthodox Church, came to lunch in my flat in Blackness Avenue. There was a tremendous feeling of serenity and holiness. I could well understand St Peter's desire to build three booths on the Mount of Transfiguration. It is an experience one wants to hang on to for as long as possible.

So when we read in St John's Gospel that Jesus breathed on his disciples and then said: "Peace be with you . . . " he wasn't uttering some vague salutation: "The Lord be with you . . . And with thy spirit . . . " No. He was imparting the gift of the Holy Spirit. The Spirit of God which gives joy, peace, love, compassion, tenderness, hope – all those things which are in such short supply in the world. Peace as a presence. Peace as a person. Something that can fill us with an inner joy and happiness – that changes us for the better.

Some of you may have bicycles. All of us have had bicycles at one time or another. And we have all experienced those sad moments when we discover that a tyre is flat and we are far from home. We need some pneuma. We need some puff. We need some air. And the strange thing is that it's all around us. Bags of it. And we know that if we're going to get anywhere on our bikes, we have to get out our pumps and start getting some pneuma into those tyres. Without it, we haven't got a hope of getting anywhere. But when it's in those tyres, we just sail away!

Right from the moment he was born, Jesus was the Prince of Peace. That is not some vague title. He was the One in whom men saw the life of God – and the power of God.

On the sea of Galilee, the disciples had to cope with a storm. It was something they were used to. They were professionals. So they battened down the hatches. They reduced the sails. They started bailing. But, we are told, it was too much for them. They started sinking. At that last despairing moment, they turned to their passenger – who was asleep! "Lord, save us!" they said. "We're perishing!" And Jesus spoke to the waves and storm: "Be still!" And there was immediately an almighty calm. And the disciples didn't know which was the more terrifying – the storm or the sudden calm. "Be still! And know that I am God."

The peace of God is the peace which passes all human understanding. The presence of God in a man or woman is incomprehensible. Why should God want to be in me? Yet it is his presence which comforts us in times of sorrow and bereavement. People say: "I don't know how I got through it. I seem to have been given extra strength to cope." Just so. God"s presence brings an end to strife. Gives us hope in place of fear. Assures us of life after death. The peace of God turns the world upside down! Wrong! The peace of God turns the world right way up!

In that Upper Room, on the first Easter day, the Risen Lord gave his peace to the disciples. He gave them life and power. He gave them something of himself – risen, ascended, glorified. He gave to them something of the life of God. Something that they could hand on and share with other people.

And so today – another Easter Day – we come to him and ask him for his help. We say: "O Lamb of God, that takest away the sins of the world, grant us thy peace."

We live in a world where is no peace. Where everyone's tyres are flat. The ride is miserable. The road is hard and we bounce from one pothole to another, not knowing where the next bump in the road will throw us. Give us some of that divine pneuma. The gift of your Spirit to help us on our journey. The politicians can't give us anything; but you can. We need to receive the breath of God – to give us life and hope and joy. If we cannot have peace in the world, we can at least have it in our hearts.

And Jesus breathed on them and said: "Receive the Holy Spirit." He also said: "Ask and you will receive."

So, ask!

(6th April 1975)

Mother Who?

The city of Norwich has a number of local heroes – among them Lord Nelson, the victor of Trafalgar; the nurse, Edith Cavell; and Elizabeth Fry, the prison reformer.

Every year, these people are honoured and remembered. But in 1973, another name was added to the list. In a joint celebration in Norwich Cathedral, attended by Anglicans and Roman Catholics, special tribute was paid to a person called Julian of Norwich.

Despite the name, it turned out that Julian was a woman! That she had lived six hundred years before. And that her name was not really Julian at all! That was simply the name of the Church where she worked. No one knows exactly when she was born or when she died. And no one in Britain had even heard of her till 1901!

So what was all the fuss about? Why celebrate the life of this unknown woman? The reason is that she wrote a book – the first book we know of to be written by a woman in English. She wrote at the same time as Geoffrey Chaucer, who penned "The Canterbury Tales." But whereas his book has been handed down the centuries as a classic of English literature, Julian's book was lost.

Presumably copies were kept in one of the thirty-two churches or twenty-two convents which flourished in medieval Norwich, but all these libraries were destroyed by King Henry VIII. He took the best books for his library and sold off or burnt the rest.

Julian's little book was in English – then the language of the peasants. It was not bound in silver or gold or written on illuminated manuscripts. Most of the copies would have perished. But two survived.

One copy found its way to the British Museum in 1753 and one was reprinted in France in 1670. Not until 1901 was her book available to the British public. Since then, over one hundred editions of that book have been published and, in 1980, this unknown Julian was commemorated as one of the few great saints of the Church of England! Fame at last!

Julian of Norwich was born sometime in 1342 and lived till she was over seventy. That in itself was quite an achievement. For her life coincided with the Black Death when one-third of the population died in twenty years. Her young life in Norwich would have been full of dreadful scenes of bodies being thrown on to carts for mass burial. It was an era of great calamities, poor harvests, hunger and the Peasants' Revolt. Churches and monasteries were attacked and looted. The Bishop of Norwich ordered the rebels to be hung, drawn and quartered.

During her lifetime, there was the unending Hundred Years War with France, the great rift in the Church with two different Popes claiming legitimacy. Not to be left out of the fun, the spire of Norwich Cathedral fell down and destroyed the eastern half of the church. John Wycliff was being ruthlessly persecuted for translating the Bible into English and many of his followers were burnt at the stake.

I describe all these unsavoury happenings in case you might think that Mother Julian was living a sheltered, peaceful, privileged life in her convent in Norwich. In fact, it was a very violent age and the violence was even on her own doorstep. But despite all the tragedies, she called her book:" Revelations of Divine Love."

It was written as a result of a series of visions she had on May 8th 1373. She had been on the point of death – almost away – and at that moment, she had a vision of God. A vision which she spent the next twenty years recording in her little book. She has a number of key points to make:

"I saw that God is to us everything that is good. He is our clothing. In his love, he wraps and holds us. He enfolds us in his love and will never let us go. As the body is clad in clothes and the flesh in skin, so we are clothed body and soul in the goodness of God and enfolded in it. No created being can comprehend how much and how sweetly and how tenderly our Maker loves us. He wills that we should strive to know him and to love him till we are made whole in heaven."

Long before ecology and "green" issues became a political hot potato, Mother Julian wrote a very up-to-date picture of creation:

"God showed me this little thing. It was the size of a hazelnut in the palm of my hand. It was as round as a ball. I looked at it with my mind's eye and thought: 'What can this be?' And the answer came back: 'It is all that is made.'

And I marvelled that it could last, for I thought it might have crumbled to nothing, it was so small. And the answer came into my mind; 'It lasts and ever shall be because God loves it.' In this little thing, I saw three truths. The first is that God made it. The second is that God loves it. The third is that God looks after it."

So how should ordinary mortals react to God's love: "It is God's will that we should rejoice with him in our salvation and that we should be cheered and strengthened by it. For we are the apple of his eye. He delights in us for ever – as we shall in him – by his grace."

The trouble is that we are not perfect, not very close to God. Sin places its daily barrier between us and God. Julian has an answer for all this:

"God showed me that sin shall not be shame to man, but a glory. For as every sin brings its own suffering, so every soul that sins shall earn a blessing by love. And just as many sins are punished with much suffering, because they are so bad, even so they shall be rewarded with many joys in heaven, because of the sorrow and suffering they have caused the soul here on earth."

How's that for a revolutionary idea! The more sins we commit, the greater the blessings in heaven. Quite the opposite to St Paul: "Shall we sin in order that grace may abound? . . . By no means!" Her belief is that all our sorrows and sadness will have a happy ending. Perhaps the most famous words that she wrote – quoted by T.S. Eliot in his poem – are these:

"The cause of all this pain is sin. But all shall be well and all shall be well. And all manner of thing shall be well. These words were said to me so kindly and without any hint of blame to me or to any who shall be saved. So how unjust it would be for me to blame God for allowing my sin when he does not blame me for falling into it."

At this moment, when there is so much going on in our Diocese that is depressing and disheartening, I think it would perhaps be helpful for all of us to hang on to these words of Mother Julian. That all shall be well and that all of us remain within the grace and protection of God our Father. "All shall be well. . ."

Which brings us to Julian's final blockbuster! Six hundred years before women's liberation was even thought of, Julian made an observation which still makes one raise one's eyebrows:

"As truly as God is our Father, so just as truly he is our Mother! I saw that God rejoices that he is our Father and God rejoices that he is our Mother and God rejoices that he is our husband and our soul is his beloved wife. And Christ rejoices that he is our brother. These are five great joys as I see it, which he wills us to delight in – praising him, thanking him, loving him and blessing him for ever."

Julian is not saying that God is a woman. The Bible tells us that God created us in his own image, both male and female. Within God's nature, there is both fatherly love and motherly love – combined. It is very important for Christians to recognize both these aspects within the nature of God. The motherliness of God is not to be underestimated or despised.

"A mother will sometimes let her child fall or suffer in various ways, so that it may learn by its mistakes. But she will never let any real harm come to the child because of her love. And though earthly mothers may not be able to prevent their children from dying, our heavenly mother, Jesus, will never let his children see death. For he is all might, all wisdom, all love."

This address contains only a small fraction of Julian's thoughts contained in her book: "Revelations of Divine Love." Might it tempt you to read more? To me, Julian is very much a saint for our times – helping us to look beyond the present squalor and misery to the glory which God has given us in his sacraments and which he has prepared for all of us in heaven. Let us never lose sight of our vision and our calling. It is so precious.

"Flee to God and you shall be comforted. Touch him and you will be made clean. Cling to him and you will be safe from all kinds of danger. For our courteous Lord wills that we should be as at home with him as heart may think or our souls desire. Utterly at home, he lives in us for ever. Amen."

(25th July 1993)

Sweet Sacrament Divine

Very often, when our Bishop is about to offer our people their communion, he says: "The things of God – for the people of God." I know what he means. But I find myself questioning the use of the word: "things." It is not a word I like. It is the sort of word I use when I have a lapse of memory . . . when my vocabulary fails . . . "You know the sort of thing I mean . . . " "The thing I was using a couple of minutes ago . . . " I think the sacraments we receive at the altar deserve a better description than: "things."

For a starter, the bread and wine which we use are not just the gifts of God's creation. They are the work of men's hands . . . women's hands . . . Human beings have harvested these gifts. They have bottled it . . . baked it. So the bread and wine which we offer at this service contain a significant human component. It is not just bread – not just wine. It comes as a result of human labour – human ingenuity. It is bread plus . . . wine plus.

And it is offered up. To whom? To our Lord himself. Jesus said: "When two or three are gathered together in my name, I am in the midst of them." One either believes this or one doesn't. But if we do believe that Jesus is in any way present at our communion service, then perhaps it makes our offering more than just habit or custom.

We talk – in our Consecration prayer – of offering up "ourselves, our souls and bodies as a holy and living sacrifice." So there is clearly more to this "offering up" than mere bread and wine. It seems that the "offering up" involves every part of us. Body, mind and spirit are all included. There is a wholeness – a totality – which is being offered. Bread plus me; wine plus me.

It is no use offering up a little bit of ourselves. A little bit of our labours. A fraction of our love. In offering up this bread and wine, we are offering up all that we have – all that we are – to God. That is what is happening on our side of the table!

But if Jesus is present – as he said he would be – what is he doing? Is he just smiling and nodding as he accepts our gift? Or is he doing something more?

We notice from reading the Gospel, that when Jesus was faced with bread – either on the shores of Lake Galilee or in a house in Emmaus – he usually blessed it and broke it. Doubtless, it was a Jewish custom. Part of their Passover tradition. But we are told that he was also recognized in the breaking of bread. There was something of himself in the action.

Jesus said; "This is my Body; this is my Blood." Extraordinary words. I am sure that he would not have said them unless he had meant them. Jesus identified himself completely with these objects of bread and wine. He invested them with significance and power. It was not just in Bethlehem that the Word became flesh and dwelt amongst us. It happens at every communion service.

145

So then, we believe that as we receive – consume – absorb – these divine objects, we are receiving a part of his resurrection life. Something of Jesus as he is today.

His power . . . his Spirit . . . his life . . . They are added to these gifts. Something precious from God dwells in us. The Church calls itself the Body of Christ – because we bear about in our daily life something of the divine nature – an inward and spiritual grace which does not come from our input – but his. Bread plus his life. Wine plus his power. Given to us.

Just as the grain of wheat is transformed into bread – and the grape into wine, so in this act of offering and receiving, there is transformation. A change in the actual gifts themselves. An act of re-creation – transforming our sinful bodies into a new creature fit for heaven.

As in all acts of creation, the transformation is not achieved overnight – with the waving of a magic wand. I think I must have heard "The Queen of Sheba" being played at least fifty times before Amy played it at our service yesterday. And Bob must have poured out much sweated labour to transform our rather ugly, tarnished processional cross into the beautiful shining object we see today.

God's re-creation of our sinful nature is part of an on-going process which may very well take a lifetime – and more – to accomplish. God dwells in us – and we in him. He is at work in us – as we work our way towards him. You see, the sacraments are not an end in themselves. They are a means of changing us – and changing the world.

One of the things that we learn as Christians is that God prefers to use ordinary things – ordinary people – to make extraordinary things happen. To offer him our gifts of bread and wine – and, with them, ourselves, our souls and bodies – is to offer the totality of our being to him. Equally, to receive his strength, life and power through these objects – duly blessed and consecrated from his side of the table – is to receive the totality of God in us.

There is already a divine presence in all creation. But as we know from bitter experience, it is very difficult for divine love to work in human beings. They seem to be built differently! God's way of cleansing and transforming us is subtle. It takes the eye of faith to see what is happening. But through this sacrament, God is at work redeeming us and saving mankind from all its folly and destruction. The sad thing is that, despite all his efforts, so little divine love percolates through.

So, at this service, the priest stands at the crossroads between the human and the divine. Standing in the middle of a crossroads is never a safe place to be! (Especially if you see a silver-coloured Metro heading your way!) It is bad enough ministering to the people of God! But to come face to face with the Risen Christ is far more daunting! Perhaps you will understand why we approach the altar with confidence and joy – but also in fear and trembling at the tremendous responsibility of the gift being placed in our hands ... deposited in our hearts.

I do not want to make James's first celebration more difficult or more glorious than it already is; but this is what we are up to – and this is why the Eucharist is so vital in our lives. "The things of God – for the people of God." So true – and yet, so much more!

(29th August 1999)

Stoned!

When the Jews were in the wilderness, they worshipped in tents. The word: "tabernacle" means a "tent." And the virtue of a tent is that when you move, your place of worship moves with you! But once they settled in the land of Israel, they wanted a more permanent place of worship. Like the pagans around them, they yearned for a temple that would express the glory, the strength and the importance of their God. And so they built this huge structure with large stones so that it would not easily be moved.

As we heard in this morning's first reading, they believed that God would be happy to live in this Temple they had built. Certainly, when Isaiah had his vision of God, it was in the Temple that he saw all the glory of the Lord – cherubim, seraphim and all the rest. But the only precious item housed in the Temple was the Ark of the Covenant – a wooden box carried on two poles. What did it contain? It contained the tablets of stone which Moses received on Mount Sinai, engraved with the Ten Commandments.

People had this great belief that if something was built of stone – or engraved in stone – it would endure. So, throughout history, people have put up plaques, pillars, statues, tombstones, arches and shrines to commemorate those they have respected, loved and valued. "Their name shall live for evermore . . . "

But it doesn't! When I went to Iona, I noticed that the inscription on John Smith's tomb had almost completely gone. The Labour leader had died seven years before, but in that time, the words had been sandblasted by rain and wind. As we know from bitter experience here in Dundee, gravestones are often vandalized – or fall over. They are moved by Council officials building a multi-storey car park. Churches and temples have been bombed, bull-dozed or attacked by Puritans or members of the Taliban. Nothing is sacred. Stone is not quite as enduring as people would like to think.

Jesus himself had little time for temples. As he told the woman beside the well in Samaria, there would soon be no temples. They would all vanish. What would people do then? When that moment comes, he said, people would worship God "in spirit and in truth." That's all that's needed!

He might have saved his breath. Christians have been even more enthusiastic than the Jews in putting up temples and shrines. Every sacred place in Jerusalem or Bethlehem has a church built over it. A woman has a vision of the Virgin Mary . . . Erect a basilica! The bigger and more ornate the better. Even our own dear Bishop Forbes was empowered by the same basic instinct. You will remember that he described his churches as "Alleluyas built in stone."

St Paul was on the right track when he described the human body as the temple for God's Holy Spirit. A weak, frail human body. There God would dwell. In us, his glory would be perceived. And if there were to be any commandments in this New Testament, they would be engraved in men's hearts – certainly not on stone.

This is what Jesus himself taught us in his Sermon on the Mount. Not a sermon in a synagogue but a sermon delivered on a hillside in Galilee. It has survived. And in our Gospel for this morning, we read of Jesus taking bread and blessing it and with it, feeding the 5000. And he managed to do it without a stone altar. Not even a holy table. No expensive props.

Buildings are expensive. The things which cost us money are stones, pipes, gutters, slates, boilers, heating, insurance. Their burden lies heavily upon us. What can we do? We live with the same dilemma which faced King Solomon: "Can God indeed live in this house which I have made? Surely the heaven of heavens cannot contain him?" And yet we still think that God will be where we want him to be.

No. We have to blow our tiny minds; to see God in the greatness of creation; in the thunder; in the power of the sea; in all things bright and beautiful. The love and power of God expressed in a thousand different ways. Our whole life is a sacrament. God dwelling in every part; close to us in even our sin and shame; in our failures and faithlessness.

So, do we need churches? Yes . . . but only if they help to bring us closer to God. Churches so often divide people into categories and classes. Them and us. Even the old St Mary Magdalene's had mission churches for the poor – the mother church was for the better off. If churches (ie. people) use their churches (ie. buildings) for the glory of God – for the worship of God, then He will be present in them – in us. But if we use our churches to promote ourselves, our riches, our talents, our power, our heroic deeds, then perhaps there will be little room left for God?

It is easy to forget that all our worship – all our prayers – are offered "through Jesus Christ our Lord." The most precious gift we receive is the Body and Blood of Christ – the Resurrection life which begins here and now; not just when we die. The real glory of the Church is God dwelling in us – giving us his power, his life, his love, all the gifts of the Spirit. All those things which make us civilized human beings. All those gifts which the world seems to lack.

Here in Scotland, we are busy building a new temple to the glory of the Scottish people. It will cost a little over £450 million pounds. Will God dwell in the new Holyrood Parliament? Or will it become a Temple of Babel and violence; of division and strife? I think we can easily guess the answer. We have seen it so many times before. The League of Nations. The United Nations. The European Parliament. All built with the best will in the world. But, ultimately, monuments to human folly.

When Elijah met God, he met him in the desert. God's message came in a still, small voice. Only if churches enable us to hear that still, small voice are they worth preserving and hallowing. Without the glory of God filling this temple, it is merely an empty shrine.

"Lord, thy glory fills the heavens;
Earth is with its fulness stored;
Unto thee be glory given,
Holy, holy, holy Lord."

(1st August 2004)

Church And State

"Let every soul be subject to the higher powers, for there is no power but of God; the powers that be are ordained of God."

It is quite clear that St Paul wrote this passage before the persecution of the Emperor Nero. He obviously believed that governments were benign. Paul was very much a child of the Augustinian age where good government was one of the principal features of the Roman Empire.

You paid your taxes. In return, you got peace and protection. You were free to trade and travel. In the last resort, you could appeal to Caesar and obtain justice from the highest court in the Empire. It is perhaps a little ironic that the Emperor to whom St Paul appealed was, in fact, Nero, the Emperor who did so much damage to the Christian Church.

I would imagine that if he had been writing ten years later an Epistle to the Romans, he might have seen things in a very different light. But, of course, by then both he and St Peter were dead – condemned by the very man he had extolled.

I would imagine that, seen close up, the Emperor Nero did not seem anything like "a minister of God." Because it wasn't just Christians whom he killed. He killed all his opponents – even his wife. At best, we might say, St Paul was wrong.

Christians rapidly discovered that secular governments were far from benign. In fact, for the first 250 years of the Church's life, there was never-ending persecution. Its leaders and its followers were killed because they would not accept the deity of the Emperor or the authority of the State.

One of the reasons why our own Scottish Episcopal Church was banned by Act of Parliament for forty-six years – the only Church in Britain to be banned by Act of Parliament – was because it would not accept the legitimacy of the House of Hanover. It continued to regard the royal House of Stuart as the true rulers of Britain – long after history had moved on. They had sworn allegiance and they believed they should keep those promises. Because they would not give way, their chapels were burnt down, their worship was forbidden and the estates of any well-to-do Episcopalians were confiscated by the State. If more than five Episcopalians worshipped together in one room, they could be fined for the first offence; jailed or deported to the colonies for any subsequent offence.

Episcopalians learnt their lesson the hard way. The price of the ban being lifted was that they should – in future – pray for the reigning King or Queen of England. Conform and all will be well. On the whole, it has worked. We do not cause the Government any trouble. In return, we live in peace and can go about our worship without any interference.

The State may not particularly like the Church . . . Remember the reaction of Mrs Thatcher and her ministers when the Church of England produced its excellent report: "Faith in the City", challenging the assumptions and policy of the Government. The knuckledusters came out! The Church was given a severe drubbing. More care was taken in the appointment of bishops. In return for a few juicy bones, the dog is expected to stay in its kennel and keep quiet.

But what happens when the Church finds itself in a hostile environment? When democracy is replaced by dictatorship? When the State imprisons its people without trial? When it kills six million Jews – or one million Tutsis? When a State starts building a nuclear reactor to make bombs? When a Government refuses to acknowledge the existence of AIDS and refuses to provide medicine for sick people? When a Government uses its power to starve its political opponents? When a Prime Minister goes to war on a fraudulent prospectus?

What does the Christian say? Or do? Does the Christian still honour and obey? Do we still sing: "God bless our gracious Queen"? Do we still pay our taxes? Dare we put our religious freedom at risk? After all, if the State turned nasty and charged business rates on Church buildings, they could break us financially. We could lose the generous Gift Aid. Historic Scotland could stop giving grants to maintain our buildings. There are many ways the State could hit back at us. They could do us more damage than we could ever do to them. So do we shut our eyes? Keep our heads down? Do we by our silence condone evil?

In history, Christians have normally been on the side of

the poor, the down-trodden, the marginalized, the persecuted. Largely because Jesus himself was on the wrong side of the barricade. Contradicting the Jewish Law. Challenging the Pharisees and Sadducees. "He has put down the mighty from their seat and exalted the humble and meek. He has filled the hungry with good things and the rich he has sent empty away."

Perhaps it is one of the Church's failings in Britain that it has not been vocal enough. It has not challenged governments, authority figures, lawyers, bishops, councillors, doctors with quite the vigour it should. It seems that the Church does not want to rock the boat. After all, in England, the Queen is the temporal head of the Church of England. The clergy are all – technically – civil servants!

In the Episcopal Church, we need have no such inhibitions. Our Church can speak its mind. We have nothing to lose. We are so small anyway. We are not part of a national church. We have no earthly leader. As St Paul said: "our citizenship is in heaven." So we do not have to bend and twist, to grovel or compromise. The Law of Love is the only thing that rules our hearts. And if we follow the path of love and forgiveness, we cannot go far wrong.

Some years ago, I was challenged over my support for the remarriage of divorced people in church. This person asked me if I thought I was doing the right thing. I said that, if I got to heaven and found that I had been wrong, I would rather be judged for doing something loving and compassionate – than for saying "No", shutting the door on a large number of unhappy people and refusing to provide pastoral help to get them back on the road to a happier married life. If we err on the side of being more loving, it can never be a sin. God himself has broken all the rules. Jesus did it all the time. It interesting to note that in the Episcopal Church, we have been remarrying divorced people for twenty-three years. In England, it is still taboo.

So then, our Epistle for this morning (Romans 13 vv 1 – 7) is an arch candidate for Room 101. To be consigned to the flames! It is not one of St Paul's inspired pieces. He got it wrong. Scripture is fallible. St Paul was misled by the peace which prevailed at the time he was writing his letter. No longer can we say that the power of God is mediated through a secular government. No one could believe for a minute that Mr Mugabe, Mr Bush, Mr Blair or Mr Chirac have been appointed God's servants – and must be obeyed. No way!

The Christian Church is here to challenge the values and politics of governments and leaders the world over. We are here to challenge our own leaders – even our own bishops and clergy. We need to be the Moral Minority – the Vocal Minority – that sees and judges. But we can only do that, if we ourselves are true to our faith. If our morals and standards are higher than theirs.

So then – we may pay taxes; we may still seek protection and peace from our rulers; we may yearn for good government. But we do not honour anyone except our Lord, the immortal, invisible and only wise God. To him be honour and glory, now and forever. Amen.

(21st August 2005)

Rejoice!

We live in a world where there are suicide bombings and Mozart's Requiem; terrorism and Michaelangelo's Pieta. Both are achievements of the human mind.

One creative, the other destructive. They stand in painful contrast. What we are – and what we might be.

It is difficult to sing when the world around you is collapsing. One thinks perhaps of Dame Myra Hess, playing in the National Gallery in Trafalgar Square, during the Second World War. All the pictures had been taken away to caves in Wales. At any moment, the Gallery might have been reduced to rubble; but every lunchtime, she gave a piano recital whilst the bombs fell and the sirens wailed.

Richard Strauss, my favourite composer, was deeply distressed by the destruction of the Munich Opera House. For him, it was the end of civilization. Did he sit down and weep? Of course he did. Did he give up? No. He sat down and wrote the hauntingly beautiful; "Metamorphosen" for twenty-three stringed instruments.

When things go wrong, should we give up? Should we let evil triumph? It is part of our human nature that we seek to rebuild. We sing through our tears. We cling on to beautiful things. St Paul captured this spirit when he wrote to the Christians in Philippi: "Rejoice in the Lord alway. And again I say: 'Rejoice!'" When the going is tough; when people say nasty things about you; when you've been stoned or shipwrecked . . . turn your mind to heaven and all its glories. "Whatever is pure; whatever is lovely; whatever is gracious . . . think about these things." It is the best medicine.

As Christians, we believe in God's creative Spirit which brings beauty out of chaos; life out of death; victory out of human misfortune. This is very obvious in the lives of the great composers. Delius was blind. Beethoven was deaf. Schubert was dying of syphilis; Schumann was approaching madness. Haydn had the French revolutionary armies at the gates of Vienna. But none of them stopped composing. Even out of the horrors of Guernica – the little town bombed in the Spanish Civil War, we have Picasso's famous picture.

Perhaps the only way we can make sense out of our tragedies is to create something beautiful. Something colourful, something melodious out of something horrible. What will the Americans create out of the disaster of September 11th?

The Bible is a record of God triumphing over human failure. Bringing slaves out of bondage; leading them to freedom in a promised land. The birth of Jesus in the very place where King Herod slaughtered the babes of Bethlehem. The glory of Easter Day following the darkness of Good Friday. Despite all the sorrows, the saints rejoice in the triumph of God over human wickedness. That is the Gospel we proclaim. A Gospel of Hope.

Bishop Kenneth Carey – formerly Bishop of Edinburgh and the man responsible for bringing me up to Scotland – once said: "Faith has been described as a great Cathedral filled with lofty visions and beautiful windows. Love as a great hospital full of care and devotion. But without hope, it would all be a great cemetery."

The Christian Church is, in itself, a vessel of hope for mankind. Despite all the things that hit us . . . Despite all the things that go wrong . . . through everything, God's creative spirit works to bring new life. But, so often, the only obstacle to God's creative spirit is the Church itself. We are all so gloomy . . . so pessimistic . . . so lacking in faith.

If we dig – just under the surface – we find many signs of hope. A few months ago, I was saying to several members of the congregation how few baptisms we had done this year. A declaration of despair! But once Andrew and I got down to visiting the parents and children, we discovered lots of people wanting baptisms for their children. There is an abundance of life waiting to be discovered. If only we start digging . . . If only we start looking . . . The Christian Church always wants to have its miracles delivered to it on a plate. But instead of expecting divine freebies, we should be willing to dig deeper.

At their recent General Assembly in Edinburgh, the Church of Scotland said: "In fifty years time, our Church will be dead!" How's that for a ringing declaration of faith! Who would want to join a Church that is on the skids? We defeat ourselves by our own negativism. A previous Rector of St Mary Magdalene's was convinced that there was no future for our Church. He said that he would see the key turn in the lock. Fortunately, the congregation did not believe him. One elderly man told me that he had prayed every day for the Church to survive. Well, it has.

Even when we are in the pits of despair – bombed out – the Christian looks for signs of hope. They are always there. No Church needs to close. Like the artist – or the musician – we have to co-operate with God's creative spirit to make things happen. To bring new life. It will come. Nikos Kazanstakis, the writer of "God's Pauper", the life of St. Francis of Assisi, said: "The canary is like man's soul. It is surrounded by bars; but instead of despairing, it sings . . . and, one day, its song will break those bars."

We have perhaps been too slow – even in St Mary Magdalene's – in making full use of this gift of hope. We are pleased to see evidence of it in other people. Nice to see the Rector so hopeful! But what about everyone else? Young and old! Should we not – all of us – be doing something beautiful for God?

Some people will say: "I'm too old. Thirty years ago, I might have had a bash; but not now." Do you not remember that God began his relationship with the Jewish people by calling Abraham – an old age pensioner – away from the sheepfolds – driving him and his family out of Ur on that great adventure of faith? He might have died on the way! But he made it. There is still a lot of zip in every pensioner. Even if you are totally housebound, you can still pray. So, pray!

In two years time, we shall be celebrating the Church's 150th Birthday. Doubtless we shall have some big display of vestments and altar frontals. We shall sell commemorative mugs and tea towels. If we are mad enough, we may float a large balloon over the church saying: "Happy Birthday". But the best present of all will be to build up the Church, bring in new people, make the place hum with life. Let us do something beautiful for God!

When others despair . . . When the ship sinks . . . When the wheels fall off the ecclesiastical wagon . . . When others say: "We've had it . . . " God says: "Rejoice!" This is a great moment to be alive! Go on hoping! Go on believing! Discover new people! Dig for victory! Let us take a leaf out of the lives of the great composers – the great artists – the men and women of faith. Even surrounded by so much death and destruction, they said: "Let us sing to the Lord a new song! Let us paint a new picture! Let us rebuild our shattered cities! Above all, let us rejoice!"

(23rd June 2002)